IMAGES
of Sports

SETON HALL
PIRATES
A BASKETBALL HISTORY

TIPOFF! The first game coached by John "Honey" Russell at Seton Hall came on December 5, 1936, when Seton Hall played the Villanova Wildcats in Philadelphia. Co-captain Dick DeLosa of Seton Hall (right) controlled this center tap. This has always been the signal to start a game, but it was eliminated in college play after each free throw and field goal made prior to the 1937–1938 season. This particular move created an average of 12 minutes additional playing time (based on the running-clock system of timekeeping in vogue during the 1930s), revolutionized the center position, and made for higher scoring tallies in the process. This game also marked the genesis of Seton Hall's move up to high-level competition and national exposure for the school. As Msgr. Robert Sheeran, the current university president, noted, this evolution has come full circle: "Athletics has been a part of education at Seton Hall from the very beginning, and across the years, but especially since the 1930s, men's basketball has emerged as one of our most impressive athletic programs." (SHU Archives.)

IMAGES
of Sports

SETON HALL
PIRATES
A BASKETBALL HISTORY

Alan Delozier

ARCADIA

Dedicated with love to Rosemary and Bernard Delozier, who are not only wonderful parents but fine individuals whose values, support, and courage have provided me with an inspirational example to live by.

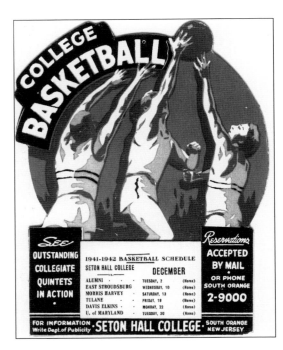

TIX FIX! As Seton Hall's court fortunes rose, so did their popularity and the demand for ducats. This 1941 promotional insert provided the opportunity for the general public to see the "Wonder Five" in action at the recently opened 2,000-plus-seat Walsh Gymnasium. The adjacent parking lot had room for 1,000 cars, but, to those opting for public transit, the bus fare from Newark was 5¢. Ticket rates ranged from $1.65 for a seat in the first six rows to general admission entry at 75¢. (SHU Archives.)

CONTENTS

ACKNOWLEDGMENTS

I wish to extend a sincere thank-you to everyone who offered assistance in the course of this project. My appreciation goes to Kate Dodds, archival associate in the Msgr. William Noé Field Archives & Special Collections Center, who is a marvel of efficiency and thoughtfulness; all Seton Hall archivists, past and present; Sr. Anita Talar, professor of library science, who has provided encouragement and helpful advice in my literary-oriented endeavors; Anthony Lee, assistant professor of library science, for his suggestions; Xueming Bao, assistant professor of library science, and Ron Myzie for technical support; and all of my faculty colleagues and the entire library staff, especially Barbara Ward of the Interlibrary Loan Department, who facilitated most of my external book requests.

A warm thank-you also goes out to Msgr. Robert Sheeran, president of Seton Hall University, who provided various quotations on the past and future of the program. In addition, I wish to thank other members of the community, especially Jeff Fogelson, athletic director; Louis Orr, head men's basketball coach; Msgr. Richard Liddy, professor of Catholic thought and culture; and Warner Fusselle, the voice of Seton Hall men's basketball, for their observations on various aspects of the sport and its history at the university. I also want to thank Marie Wozniak, assistant athletic director for communications, who allowed for usage of select photographs and her donation of research material over the years. A huge thank-you also goes to photographer S.R. Smith, who generously allowed for permission to reprint various images from his collection.

I also want to thank Richie Regan, special assistant to the vice president, who provided contact leads and historical information in regard to the team; Joseph Del Rossi, director of Pirate Blue, for his encouragement and help with background issues; Susan Diamond and Frank Fleischman of the Seton Hall Public Relations Office; David Foster, associate professor of philosophical theology, and Anthony Haynor, assistant professor of sociology, for their editorial work. For their support, I also want to thank Matt Borowick, Msgr. Edward Fleming, Michael Oakes, Robyn Andreula, Karen McNanna, Bill Blanchard, and Michelle Parence.

Other individuals provided invaluable assistance, including Greg Tobin, who gave key advice on the dynamics of publishing and formatting; Naoma Welk, whose generosity and own book on South Orange has provided a wonderful model to work from; Cynthia Bee-Farley for permission to use quotations from the Chip Hilton series, and Robert Blackwell of the Newark Public Library for his investigative research. A wealth of oral history was offered through the kindness of former players and personalities, including Msgr. William Daly, Sid Dorfman, Mal Duffy, Dewey and Otto Graham, John Ligos, James Paxson, Jim Reynolds, Arnie Ring, Frank Saul, and Greg Tynes.

I wish to thank my incredible brother and sister (and fellow Atlantic 10 Conference devotees), Greg Delozier and Amy Delozier, for their fortitude and inspiration, along with my parents, Rosemary and Bernard Delozier, who are all simply wonderful and generous people!

I thank the staff at Arcadia Publishing, especially Tiffany Howe, who was most generous with her time, editing skill, and expertise in all aspects of this project.

Lastly, kudos go to the fictional Chip Hilton (modeled on former Seton Hall star Bob Davies), who asked coach Rockwell about the virtues of writing the great American game and was told, "If you really want to write basketball, go over to the public library. You'll find all the official basketball guides there. . . . You'll find records and oddities and all kinds of story material in those little books. They've got all the material you need, all the good stuff." With much enthusiasm, Chip responded, "That sounds like a *swell* idea." I agree that basketball history is a swell thing indeed. Thank you for reading.

INTRODUCTION

Seton Hall University adopted the game of basketball nearly 100 years ago, and it has become a popular fixture on campus among the student body, school administration, alumni, and all loyal rooters of the White and Blue ever since. The first official contest in school history occurred on December 9, 1903, when the Seton Hall five tied a local team, known as the Mohawks of Newark, 15-15. They scored their first win 10 days later against Brooklyn High School 28-18. Despite this early success, the program was discontinued, and a varsity squad was not fielded until five years later.

After resuming play during the 1908–1909 campaign, Seton Hall began a streak of excellence that resulted in 10 straight winning seasons (including an undefeated mark of 4-0 in 1910–1911) prior to 1918–1919, when World War I caused a second break in the schedule. During the early part of the 20th century, the college featured various head coaches, including William Caffrey, Jim Flanagan, Dick McDonough, and the renowned Frank Hill. Counted among the most prolific sideline leaders in New Jersey history, Hill piloted Seton Hall teams from 1911–1929 and posted a 191-75-1 record in the process.

The Seton Hall basketball quintets of the early 1900s played their first home games on campus at Alumni Hall or at more spacious armories and gymnasiums around the Newark area. Continued top-notch play by such cagers as John Outwater, Les Fries, and Pat Reynolds defined the style of successful South Orange teams from 1920–1922 that had a combined record of 37 wins and 9 losses in three years. Playing a largely regional slate of opponents, it was not until 1925, when Seton Hall scored its first major win by defeating Eastern Eight powerhouse Yale 33-29, that widespread recognition was earned for the program.

A milestone in school history came in 1931, when the college adopted its enduring nickname "Pirates," which was applied to all future Seton Hall basketball teams. On the court during the early to mid-1930s, Seton Hall's basketball fortunes fluctuated as various tacticians, including Dan Steinberg, Les Fries, and John Colrick, assumed the head coaching post between 1930 and 1936. The arrival of John "Honey" Russell in 1936 was a pivotal event in school history, and the Pirates achieved national prominence during his tenure, including a 295-129 record over an 18-year span (1936–1943 and 1949–1960). Included in this tally is a 41-game winning streak that led to the second undefeated season in school history (19-0 in 1939–1940) and a place in the Setonia basketball record books.

The first permanent basketball facility on campus, known as Walsh Gymnasium, opened in 1941. This structure played host to the 1939–1942 squads and featured a quintet forever known as the "Wonder Five," led by All-American Bob Davies, which brought Seton Hall its first-ever National Invitational Tournament (NIT) bid in 1941. Although the Pirates were not selected for postseason action, the team posted a combined 32-5 record over the next two years prior to the outbreak of World War II. Thereafter, they played a curtailed schedule that lasted until 1946.

Under head coaches Bob Davies and Jack Reitemeier, Seton Hall attained a 58-15 mark and three winning seasons between 1946 and 1949. These postwar Pirates were led by future National Basketball Association (NBA) stars Frank "Pep" Saul, John Macknowski, and Bobby Wanzer. Seton Hall became a prime attraction at the famed Madison Square Garden around this time, having earned its second-ever NIT bid during the 1950–1951 campaign. They followed this up with another postseason birth and 25-3 record in 1951–1952. The apex of Pirate basketball came in 1953, when Seton Hall, led by Richie Regan and All-American Walter Dukes, defeated longtime rival St. John's University to win the NIT with a 31-2 mark and a year-ending rank of second in the nation. Afterward, the Pirates were able to rally and put together a 20-win season in 1955–1956 and three straight NIT appearances between 1955 and 1957.

With the departure of Honey Russell following the 1959–1960 season, Richie Regan assumed leadership of the Pirates a year later. A point-shaving scandal in 1961 rocked the program, but Regan led the team back to respectability and winning records of 15-9 (twice), 16-7, and 13-12 between 1960 and 1964. These teams had the assistance of such performers as All-American Nick "the Quick" Werkman, who was the leading collegiate point maker nationwide in 1963. The late 1960s featured many excellent performances and players who served as a prelude to the Bill Raftery era, which began in 1970. Seton Hall returned to the NIT in 1974 and sported a succession of winning seasons between 1973 and 1979 under the playmaking of such court stalwarts as Glenn Mosley, Greg Tynes, Danny Callandrillo, and Howard McNeil.

Seton Hall became a charter member of the Big East Conference in 1979. After Horace "Hoddy" Mahon took over on an interim basis in 1982, the hiring of P.J. Carlesimo came at a time when the Meadowlands Arena and competitive league play became synonymous with the Seton Hall basketball experience. The first winning record posted by Carlesimo came during the 1986–1987 campaign when a 15-14 mark and NIT banner were earned. In 1988, Seton Hall went 22-13 and made it into the second round of the program's very first National Collegiate Athletic Association (NCAA) Tournament appearance. Another high point in the hoop annals of Setonia was recorded in 1989, when the Pirates won the Great Alaska Shootout and Sugar Bowl Tournament prior to making a run at the NCAA title. They lost the tournament to the University of Michigan 80-79 in overtime of the championship game. The Pirates compiled a 31-7 mark during the year and tied the highest win total in school history.

Between 1990 and 1994, the Pirates posted three consecutive 20-win seasons, two Big East regular season and tournament titles, an NCAA Elite Eight appearance in 1991, and Sweet Sixteen showing a year later. The 1992–1993 season featured a 28-7 record, second-round appearance in the NCAA Tournament, and a sixth rank in the season-ending polls under the play of such high scorers as Terry Dehere, Jerry Walker, and Luther Wright. Head coach George Blaney led the Pirates into the first round of the NIT in 1995 before his departure two years later. This led the way to the hiring of Tommy Amaker, who guided Seton Hall to three NIT invitations between 1997 and 2001 along with another NCAA Sweet Sixteen appearance in 2000. Seton Hall remains one of the premier basketball programs in the nation, and Louis Orr, head coach who joined the school during the 2001–2002 season, will guide the Pirates into future court battles. With the past as a prologue, I hope you enjoy this volume that recounts the memorable players, personalities, challenges, and championships that constitute the distinguished story that is Seton Hall University basketball.

GAME DAY. This is a spectator's perspective of an early-season Seton Hall contest at Walsh Gymnasium during the early 1990s. Although it no longer serves as the primary home court for the men's team, the gymnasium is the citadel of Seton Hall basketball history. (S.R. Smith and SHU Sports Information.)

One

FOUNDATION
1903–1940

THE STARTING FIVE. The 1903–1904 team was the first ever to represent Seton Hall in varsity competition 12 years after the game of basketball was invented by Dr. James Naismith in Springfield, Massachusetts. Seton Hall's earliest cagers are pictured before their inaugural game on December 9, 1903, when they tied the Mohawks of Newark club team 15-15. From left to right are the following: (front row) Martin J. Reynolds, John E. Holton (manager), and Bernard L. Stafford; (back row) William Baird, Henry "Harry" McDonough (captain), and Robert J. Barrett. Members of the team not pictured are Charles O'Neill, Francis Reilly, John Stafford, and Charles Tichler. The White and Blue ended this landmark campaign with a 2-3-1 record (varying records show that the team might have attained a 3-2-1 mark, but that has yet to be authenticated), which included a win in the last game of the season over the nearby West End Club 22-16 on January 16, 1904. (SHU Archives.)

DATE- Feb 19, 1903		PLACE Hall			G.	F.	P.
Hall		Brooklyn HS					
D.Stafford, RF		b.Stafford, Lmck					6
J.Stafford, LF		Kelchie					9
Baird, C		Connelly					0
McDonald, RR		O'Connell					9
Reynolds, LL		Mackay					0
O'Neill							
							18
Hall			14		14	28	
Brooklyn			9		9	18	

OFFICIALS- Bayle, Hennessey

INITIAL SUCCESS. The first documented home game and victory in Seton Hall history is evidenced in this early box score, which illustrates a well-balanced attack of 14 points per half en route to a 28-18 win over Brooklyn High School. Although more than 100 colleges and universities fielded basketball squads during the early 20th century, contests between academic institutions and local YMCAs, club teams, and high schools was commonplace. Despite early encouragement, the school dropped its varsity program from 1905 to 1908. (SHU Archives.)

THE FIRST WINNING SEASON. The 1908–1909 team took to the court after a three-year hiatus and posted a 10-4 mark and Seton Hall's first winning season. Under the direction of the school's first official coach (and substitute player) William Caffrey, the White and Blue posted triumphs over St. Benedict's Preparatory School 20-18, the Tiger Athletic Club 45-6, St. Francis College 34-14 and 28-18, and Cathedral College 21-16 (the first game played against a fellow college quintet). Teammates included John Clark (right forward), John Ferry (left forward), Thomas "Mussy" Herron (substitute), Henry Lynch (center), Edward McDonough (left guard), George McDonough (right guard). Other players during the 1908–1912 period included John Birchell, Otto Boltz, James Byrne, Bill Connors, Daniel Dugan, James "Steamer" Flanagan, William Maguire, and Aloysius "Bip" O'Connor. (SHU Archives.)

ALUMNI HALL. Built in 1883 at the request of Rev. James H. Corrigan, the fifth president of Seton Hall, this brownstone edifice served as home to the Alumni Association and functioned as a combination library, reading room, recreation room, and gymnasium. During the 19th century, all sporting events were scheduled and funds were raised by the Seton Hall Athletic Association. Prior to the emergence of Alumni Hall, sports-related endeavors, including football, track, baseball, handball, and cycling, were all contested outdoors. Basketball became the first indoor exercise at the college and dominated as the 20th century progressed. The building still stands and currently serves as the Immaculate Conception Seminary Chapel. (SHU Archives.)

HOME COURT ADVANTAGE. The first basketball venue on campus was found on the second floor of Alumni Hall, where games were played on a regular basis until 1923. This surface was later converted into a physics lab, but the white striped baselines remained on the floor for several years thereafter. A building known as the College Gymnasium (later Marshall Library) became home to the team until 1941. This interim site was described in the 1931 school catalog as "a large assembly hall, affords Gymnasium facilities, including an excellent basketball court." The few dozen fans who could squeeze into this arena witnessed such innovations as the zone defense, passing play, and the dribble, which promoted ball movement and offensive playmaking options as never before. (SHU Archives.)

THE PREP SQUAD. When Seton Hall College was founded in 1856, the school had a seven-year curriculum that was broken down into preparatory and collegiate divisions. The Seton Hall Preparatory School proper was established as a separate institution in 1897 but retained close ties with the college in terms of academic mission and basketball operations alike. Such figures as Richie Dec, Walter Dukes, Dick Hammock, Bo Hartmann, Mel Knight, John Outwater, Harry Renner, Frank Saul, and many other players, coaches, and support staff have represented both schools over the years. The 1911 preparatory five and subsequent teams between the second decade of the 20th century and the 1940s often played the opening game of doubleheaders featuring the Seton Hall College varsity before latter-day freshmen or women's squads assumed this position. (SHU Archives.)

YOUNG SETONIA. The 1912–1913 Seton Hall College squad was made up entirely of freshmen (three in the starting lineup) and sophomore players. Pictured, from left to right, are the following: (front row) Thomas Nugent (guard) and Gerald Kerrigan (forward); (middle row) Frank McQuade (guard), Frank Flarity (captain-center), and Peter Jones (forward); (back row) Jack Fish (forward), Edward Regley (manager), and James Byrne (guard). This team earned an 11-3 record and big wins over the University of Maryland 42-21, Drexel 52-14, and Bucknell 22-16. Seton Hall also defeated Georgetown University. The following is an account of the game: "In a game of basketball, in which free throws played a prominent part, the Seton Hall varsity team disposed of . . . Georgetown . . . last night by a score of 24 to 20. . . . No less than thirty-eight fouls were committed, each team making nineteen. The game was played under intercollegiate rules." Jones, who also played baseball, was elected to the Seton Hall Athletic Hall of Fame in 1979. (SHU Archives.)

THE 1914–1915 TEAM. This squad posted a 15-2 record and earned wins over Fordham University 39-14, George Washington 47-26, St. John's 20-18, and the Montclair Holy Name Club 58-31. However, the biggest victory came in January 1915, when Seton Hall defeated the Morristown YMCA (consisting of former collegiate stars) 110-25, the first 100-plus-point game in school history. This particular win and those recorded during the 1913–1914 season (14-3-1) were due in part to a rule change that eliminated free-for-all scrambles for balls heading out of bounds. Team members included Robert Brennan, Timothy Coughlin, Frank Cummings, Frank Flarity (captain-forward), Thomas Hannon, Ed Heine (guard), Pete Jones (forward), James McAvoy (manager), Thomas McCarthy, Frank "Stretch" Meehan (center), John Nuberg, Tom Nugent (guard), Alex Ormsby (guard), and Jim Somers (forward). (SHU Archives.)

THE 1916–1917 TEAM. Following up on a 13-3 record the previous year, the 1916–1917 squad went 12-3 and had a spotless home ledger with victories over St. Francis 46-25, Georgetown 18-17, Lafayette College 32-20, the University of Connecticut 34-19, and Galludet 49-23. Pictured, from left to right, are the following: (front row) Joe Igoe (forward), James Sommers (captain-forward), Eddie Heine (guard), and William Sullivan (guard); (back row) Matthew Fitzsimons (manager), Charles Gallagher (substitute), Michael McDonnell (substitute), Henry Coppinger (substitute), Robert Brennan (substitute), and Thomas McCarthy (substitute). The White and Blue of 1916–1917 employed an off-season training regimen, which included hiking and roller-skating around nearby Lake Hopatcong. (SHU Archives.)

"STRETCH" MEEHAN. Affectionately called "Daddy Long-Legs," Francis Meehan measured six feet six inches tall and played the center position, where he averaged eight points per game. Discovery came when coach Hill saw him strolling across campus during the fall of 1914 and literally dragged him into the gymnasium. Unfortunately, he found that he did not have a uniform that fit Meehan's massive frame! Meehan was known as the "tallest basketball player in captivity" in an era when big men were a rarity. He caused a sensation when a game with Cathedral College in 1918 was cancelled due to a dispute over his eligibility. Upon graduation in 1919, Meehan became one of the first former Seton Hall players in the professional ranks when he joined the Original Celtics and various Eastern League teams over the next few years. (SHU Archives.)

OFF-CAMPUS COURTS. Due to the limited capacity of Alumni Hall and the College Gymnasium, Seton Hall played many of their home games at various venues throughout northern New Jersey before the completion of Walsh Gymnasium in 1941. The first documented off-campus game was held on December 10, 1909, at YMCA Hall in neighboring Newark. Seton Hall also took the court at Newark Armory, Home Canal Hall, and Shanley Gymnasium. Other places used during the early years included the Orange Armory, Elizabeth Armory, and Dickinson High School in Jersey City among others. Columbia High School in Maplewood (pictured here) played host to the Pirates when they beat local rival St. Peter's College 33-17 on January 24, 1936. (SHU Archives.)

Seton Hall College Athletic Association
VARSITY BASKETBALL
1922—1923

JAS. M. COYLE	LESLIE FRIES	FRANK J. HILL
Manager	Captain	Coach

DATE		OPPONENT	PLAYED AT	Scores	
				Col.	Opp.
DECEMBER					
Sat.	9	N. Y. Training	So. Orange	38	19
Wedn.	13	St. Michael's	So. Orange		
Sat.	16	Cooper Union	So. Orange		
Fri.	29	Holy Cross	Newark		
JANUARY					
Sat.	6	Phil. Den. Col.	So. Orange		
Fri.	12	Lebanon Valley	So. Orange		
Wedn.	17	Cathedral	New York	10	42
Sat.	20	Brooklyn Law.	So. Orange	45	35
FEBRUARY					
Thurs.	1	Loyola	So. Orange	No Game	
Sat.	3	Temple Univ.	So. Orange		30
Wedn.	7	Cathedral	So. Orange		21
Tues.	13	St. Joseph Col.	Philadelphia		
Wedn.	14	Temple Univ.	Philadelphia		35
Tues.	20	Villa Nova	Villa Nova	No Game	
Thurs.	22	Northeastern C.	So. Orange		
Wedn.	28	Villa Nova	Newark	No Game	
MARCH					
Thurs.	8	Alumni	Newark		

Prep. Game will precede Varsity Game
Time of Game, 8:00 P. M.

SCHEDULING SAVVY. After World War I, Seton Hall put together three successive winning seasons (10-3 in 1919–1920, 13-4 in 1920–1921, 13-5 in 1921–1922) with such players as Jiggs Donohue, Joe Flynn, Butch McDonough, and Joe McGeer. The seasons between 1919 and 1922 included wins over St. Lawrence 38-14 (1919), Cooper Union 33-18 (1920), Brown 77-49 (1921), Northeastern 49-29 (1922), and a 2-0 forfeit victory over Manhattan College on January 18, 1922, which was awarded to Seton Hall by referee Pinky Pengitore when the Jaspers captain refused to leave the court after fouling out. The 1922–1923 team went 8-3 on the year. Starring for Frank Hill's squad were John Brown, Joe Colrick, John Corrigan, Les Fries, John Halloran, George McGovern, John Mullvaney, Peter Mooney, and Frank Porter. (SHU Archives.)

FRANK HILL. Coach Hill is credited with co-conceiving the bounce pass and pivot turn, which helped revolutionize the sport. Hill played in more than 3,000 professional games during the 1890s and early 1900s before embarking on a coaching career. He led St. Benedict's Preparatory School from 1903 to 1921, and these Grey Bee squads tallied over 10,000 points en route to an overall 209-28 record. In addition, Hill also coached at Seton Hall Preparatory, Rutgers College, and Seton Hall College, a feat made all the more amazing because he guided each program at various junctures simultaneously! Hill piloted Seton Hall College from 1911 to 1929, during which time he amassed a 191-75-1 record (.715 winning average) with only one losing season. When Seton Hall played intrastate rival Rutgers before 3,000 fans for the first time in 1924, Hill (who had a conflict of interest) only wanted a fair game and pulled for both teams to do their best. This attitude also helped Hill when served as a basketball referee for 35 years and stressed clean play in the contests he officiated. His credo at Seton Hall and beyond was, "A clean body is the result of a clean heart." Captain Joseph Schaaf of the University of Pennsylvania during the 1920s added, "Everybody hereabouts knows that Frank Hill is the last word in basketball." (SHU Archives.)

LESLIE FRIES. Nicknamed "Cap" and "Friesy," Leslie Fries gained campus fame as a special events speaker and vocalist for the glee club. Fries was another in a long line of Setonia athletes who played multiple sports and was so adept that he earned the captaincy of the basketball, baseball, and track teams in 1924. With his rallying cry of "Steady up now boys, get your man," Fries, a three-time captain of the basketball team (1922–1924), registered 509 career points and had his crowded hour on December 22, 1921, when he scored 47 points against Brown University, which stood as a school record for 42 years. He was elected to the Seton Hall Athletic Hall of Fame in 1974. (SHU Archives.)

THE 1923–1924 TEAM. This squad went 6-7 for the year and recorded victories over traditional rivals St. John's 36-35, Manhattan 35-22, St. Bonaventure 38-31, and Niagara 58-28. Players included John Brown, Tom Clohosey, Joe "Big Shot" Colrick (who rallied the boys with cries of "Give me five"), John Dwyer, Les Fries (co-captain), James "Shamus" Holleran, Mike Hornak, John Outwater (co-captain), Cyril Pruczinsky, Francis Reynolds, Joseph Ryan, and Francis Walsh. The following year, many of the same players were still in uniform and contributed to an 8-6 mark. (SHU Archives.)

SETON HALL TAMES YALE BULLDOG IN SENSATIONAL COURT BATTLE AT ARMORY

Newark is no place for a savage bulldog to run wild in and Yale, as it prepares to open its intercollegiate season with Penn tomorrow night in Philadelphia, sadly realizes that fact.

For forty minutes the white-jerseyed bouncers from New Haven sought valiantly to retain their court prestige in a sensational battle at Newark Armory—and failed. When the Bulldog had snarled and growled and spent its attack Seton Hall crashed through with another of its rallies and ran its colors to the mizzen top. The score was 33 to 29.

The game last night was a replica of the one between the Elis and Newark A. C. Monday night with the same ultimate result—Yale was unable to maintain its own terrific pace. Outstanding in old Setonia's much desired victory was the stocky figure of Jack Outwater, the basket-ball and baseball star, who still has only a junior's privileges in school.

When Yale was at the peak of its charge it was Outwater who rallied his teammates to new efforts. And when Yale, with about fifteen minutes to go, started a fresh attack with the entrance into the game of Captain Frank Lackey, it was Outwater who speared the Blue net with a long field goal that started Seton Hall on the way to victory. Outwater received wonderful assistance from "Stick" Hen by, the towering center, and valuable aid from Ryan, Hornak and Nellingan, but he came through with goals when most needed. He scored thirteen of Seton Hall's thirty-three points.

To beat famous old Yale in any

that in their final scores. Each five accounted for eleven field goals.

Jones, who started in place of Captain Lackey at forward, tossed in the first field goal on a neat pass under the basket. After Menaby had missed a foul Ryan tied the count with a field goal for Seton Hall. Breck's foul put Yale ahead again. Simmons' field goal and foul gave the Blue an 8 to 2 lead. Fouls by Hornak and Nelligan and a field tally by Outwater pulled Seton Hall up and from that point on the fives battled evenly and at half time was deadlocked, 14 to 14.

Yale gained the lead at the re-start, lost it and once again went ahead when Lackey, just rushed into the game, tallied a field goal which made the score 22 to 21 in Yale's favor. Ryan's goal from the side put Seton Hall ahead for the last time.

Henaby, Pruzinski and Outwater scored in a row before Jones sunk one for Yale. Toward the end Outwater scored a spectacular goal from the side of midcourt.

In a preliminary tilt St. Michael's of West Hoboken, tripped up the Seton Hall Prep Five, 23 to 19. A forty piece band from the Catholic Protectory in Arlington played during both tilts.

Yale	G.	F.	F.		Seton Hall	G.	F.	F.
Breck, f...	2	1	5		Outwater, f.	4	6	1
Jones, f...	3	2	9		Nellingan, f.	0	1	1
Lackey, f...	2	1	5		Henaby, c...	3	0	0
Simmons, c.	4	2	10		Ryan, g...	1	0	
Carmody, g.	0	0	0		Hornak, g..	2	5	
Frankel, g.	0	0	0		Pruzinski, f.	1	0	
Totals...	11	7	19		Totals...	11	11	82

Wow Bow! Yale University played in the first modern intercollegiate contest when they defeated the University of Pennsylvania 32-10 in 1897. The Bulldogs were also charter members of the Eastern Eight (forerunner to the Ivy League), which was an early-20th-century version of the Atlantic Coast Conference (ACC). Seton Hall was only a northern New Jersey phenomenon during its first couple of decades of basketball competition, but they defeated other future Ivy League schools, including the University of Pennsylvania (freshmen) and Dartmouth University. These were a prelude to December 30, 1925, when Seton Hall beat the "Eli" of Yale 33-29 before a sellout crowd of 3,000 at the Newark Armory and hundreds who listened at home over radio station WBPI. (SHU Archives.)

He's a Big Man at Seton Hall

FRANCIS (PAT) REYNOLDS, SETON HALL BASKETBALL ACE

FRANCIS "PAT" REYNOLDS. Reynolds was a South Orange native who stood six feet three inches tall and was a three-year starter for the varsity team, as well as president of the Setonian Club. He also showed his athletic talent as a fullback on the college football team and catcher and outfielder on the baseball team. In addition, Reynolds holds the dubious distinction of earning a varsity letter from Rutgers when he inadvertently sunk a basket in their 1924 tilt. The crowd cheered, and his deed was "rewarded" a few days later when a red sweater featuring a huge R came in the mail. Reynolds was elected to the Seton Hall Athletic Hall of Fame in 1982. (SHU Archives.)

JOHN OUTWATER. The star of numerous court wars, John Outwater was named team captain twice during the early 1920s and led Seton Hall scorers with 115 points in 1925–1926. Outwater was not only a forward on the basketball team but also pitched for the baseball team over four seasons between service as an assistant coach for the Bayley Hall Preparatory School basketball squad. In addition, Outwater also had an appointment as associate editor for the school newspaper known as the *Setonian*, which began publication in 1924. After graduation, he entered Immaculate Conception Seminary and joined the priesthood. Tragically, Father Outwater died in an automobile accident on December 27, 1936, but was elected posthumously to the Seton Hall Athletic Hall of Fame in 1976. (SHU Archives.)

THE 1925–1926 TEAM. This squad posted a 7-5 record including wins over St. Francis 38-15, Brooklyn Polytechnic 44-12, Philadelphia Osteopathy 32-28, and Drexel 25-21. Included in this team picture are Edward Colrick (guard), John Connolly (athletic association president), Thomas Grant (assistant manager), Frank Henaby (center), William Hornak (guard), Martin Liddy (guard), Leo Mahoney (manager), Raymond Nelligan (forward), John Outwater (forward), James Phelan (center), and Cyril Pruczinsky (guard). These individuals heard such helpful instructions from coach Hill as "What have you got a head for?" and "You big string-bean, you ought to be able to make that basket easier than any other member of the team," as well as "Never stop playing until that whistle blows." (SHU Archives.)

19

THE 1926–1927 TEAM. This contingent went 10-3 for the season. From left to right are the following: (front row) Stephen Mickevich (forward) and Francis Donnelly (guard); (middle row) Saul "Sol" Naidorff (guard), Willie A. Hornak (guard), Jack Outwater (captain-forward), Francis "Styx" Henaby (center), and Ray Nelligan (forward); (back row) Thomas G. Grant (manager), Robert A. Coyle (forward), Thomas J. Holleran (forward), John Griffin (center), Martin "Marty" Liddy (guard), John Blewitt (guard), and John R. Enright (assistant manager). Interestingly, Martin Liddy was the uncle of Msgr. Richard Liddy, who sold tickets to games in the early 1950s and became co-chaplain for the Pirates in the mid-1990s. (SHU Archives.)

THE 1927–1928 TEAM. This quintet went 9-4 and registered major wins over Cooper Union 48-18, Providence 38-19, St. Francis 22-21, St. Joseph's 40-21, and Drexel 25-23. Counted among the players on this team were Salvatore Basile, John R. Enright (manager), John Gallagher, John Griffin, Francis Henaby, Thomas Holleran, Joseph Maher, Stephen Michevich, James E. Naughton (assistant manager), Raymond Nelligan (captain), Cyril Pruczinsky, Walter Reilly, Harry Singleton, and Michael Torpey. Not pictured is Andy Watts, the first varsity trainer who kept each player well braced for game play under their bulky knee pads and long stockings worn during that era. (SHU Archives.)

THE MINIMS. This is the early equivalent of a freshman, rookie, or developmental squad. Made up of players from the lower school of Seton Hall, the Minims and another group tabbed the "Mosquitoes" were both created by coach Hill as a means of providing opportunities for several players of varying grade-level experience. The Minims of 1925–1926, shown here, include Michael Torpey (coach), Louis Cannizzaro (forward), Lawrence Lucey (forward), John Budnick (guard), Kenneth McNeil (captain), William O'Keefe (manager), George Mickevich (center), Edward Fallenstein (center), and Michael Atrash (guard). (SHU Archives.)

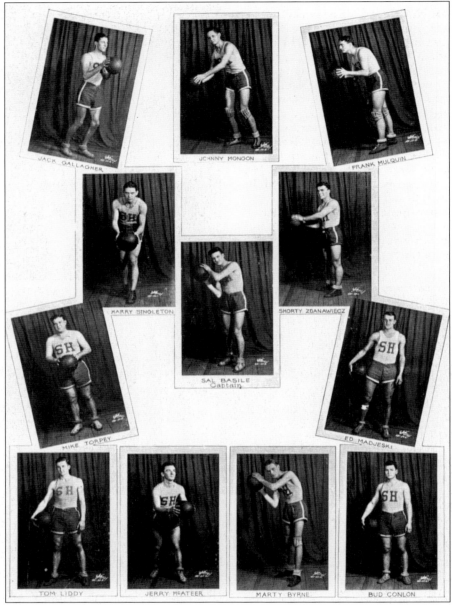

JACK GALLAGHER   JOHNNY MONOON   FRANK MULQUIN

HARRY SINGLETON   SHORTY ZBANAWIECZ

SAL BASILE
Captain

MIKE TORPEY   ED MADJESKI

TOM LIDDY   JERRY McATEER   MARTY BYRNE   BUD CONLON

THE 1929–1930 TEAM. This team, led by student council president, captain, and high scorer (153 total) Sal Basile, went 13-9 in the course of Seton Hall's first 20-plus game schedule. The 1930 team was one of the last teams to bear the name White and Blue as a college nickname before the Seton Hall–Holy Cross baseball game of April 24, 1931, which prompted a Worcester sportswriter to exclaim, "That Seton Hall team is a gang of Pirates!" (Buccaneers later became an alternate nickname.) The tag has stuck from that day forward. Another innovation came in 1930–1931, when Seton Hall adopted an early version of the "run and gun," known in that day as the Western (or racehorse) style. The team's head coach, Dan Steinberg, was a disciple of this style as a player at Lawrence College in Appleton, Wisconsin. This style helped the school attain a 13-9 (3 game results missing) record that season. (SHU Archives.)

WILLIAM NOÉ FIELD. "Father Field" was a lifelong South Orange native who was affiliated with Seton Hall from 1928 until his death in 2000, first as a student and graduate. He was later ordained as a priest and elevated to the rank of monsignor for the Archdiocese of Newark. Monsignor Field also taught English, wrote poetry, and served as director of the university library and archives at various times during his tenure at Seton Hall. Even though he ran track and was the class baseball manager at Seton Hall Preparatory, he was a basketball fan and the first season ticket holder when Walsh Gymnasium opened in 1941. He became a longtime spectator and spiritual advisor to the team. He was inducted as an honorary member of the Seton Hall Athletic Hall of Fame in 1984. (SHU Archives.)

THE 1932–1933 TEAM. This squad recorded an 8-4 record (10-9 mark in 1931–1932) and was led by former Seton Hall player and second-year coach Les Fries. The team consisted of Louis Babiak, Myron Eslar, Les Fries (head coach), Edward Hoffman, Pat McCormack, Frank McCullough, Harry McTague (manager), Robert Morgan, William Piga (assistant manager), Charles Reilly, Edward Skeuse, and John "Shorty" Zdanewicz (captain). There was no team in 1933–1934 due to academic prioritization and financial considerations, but the school featured a class titled Theory and Practice of Coaching, which was offered through the Department of Physical Education. (SHU Archives.)

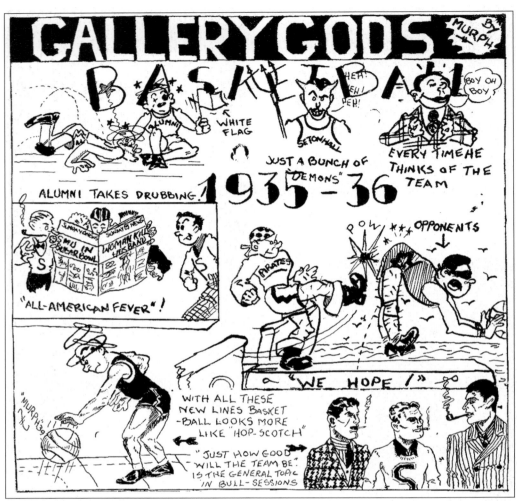

COURT WIT. This illustrative salute to Seton Hall hoopsters from the *Setonian* showed affection in the face of affliction even with a 4-11 record in 1934–1935. Along with chic caricatures, odes to campus cagers held sway in the student press. A poem entitled "The Pirates," penned by Thomas J. Gillhooly, appeared in the April 1931 *Setonian* and proclaimed, "Our teams are known as Pirates, In the world where sport holds sway; And like their honored forbears, Nothing stands in their way. . . . In the realms of basketball, The Pirates stand supreme; For here is their initial charge, Their booty . . . so it seems. . . . On, onward to greater heights, In the world where sport holds sway; And where your honored forbears, Pridefully bless your day." During 1935, the modern three-second rule went into effect, and the team scored upon was able to place the ball back into play under its own basket instead of facing the fate of a jump ball after each field goal as before. (SHU Archives.)

24

HONEY. On November 24, 1936, John "Honey" Russell was named head coach of the Seton Hall Pirates. Russell's first year at the helm ended in a 5-10 mark (and a bachelor of science degree), but this only served as a harbinger to greater success and his status as the all-time winningest basketball coach in Seton Hall history. As Russell noted in a December 1936 interview, "To say that my initial experiences as basketball coach at Seton Hall have been unique, interesting, and most pleasant would be putting it mildly." Russell also played professionally from 1919 to 1945 and appeared in over 3,200 games for such teams as the New York Jewels and Cleveland Rosenblums. An early advocate of the city game, Russell endorsed this style of play that included tough defense and accurate shooting, which helped when he became the first coach of the Boston Celtics from 1946 to 1948. Msgr. James Kelley (president of Seton Hall College from 1936 to 1949), who hired Russell, also paid him high praise: "Russell was the most honest man I ever met. . . . He never yelled at a referee and was respected by everyone. He was sharp, smart, able to turn almost anything to an advantage for his team." (SHU Archives.)

CHEERY-O! From spirited arm flailing to megaphone thumping, cheerleading is designed to whip crowds into a frenzy. Many of Seton Hall's most enduring cheers, such as "S-E-T-O-N-I-A" and "The White and Blue," were written by Joseph Toohey, John Sullivan, and Joseph Dooling in the mid-1920s. Members of the 1936–1937 yell squad include John Howe, Joe Beggans, Dick Holmes, and Horton Ranght. (SHU Archives.)

A PEP RALLY. The lighting of a symbolic season-beginning bonfire was a Seton Hall tradition during the early years of the program. This particular pyre was lit on December 3, 1936, and guarded by various students from the preparatory school and college. As the 1931 *Setonian* featured in one of its editorial outbursts on the subject, "The support must be universal—it must be whole-hearted, voluntary, enthusiastic; it must be support that endures in defeat as well as in victory—this and nothing else is implied by the 'support of college athletics . . . Setonians!'" (SHU Archives.)

GAME CAPTAINS. Co-captains Dick "Lank" DeLosa and Ed McNally of Seton Hall flank J. Brennan of Villanova as they meet at midcourt prior to a game on December 5, 1936. This contest came in the wake of back-to-back 4-11 campaigns between 1934 and 1936 under head coach John Colrick and such players as Dennis Buttimore, Stanley Ostaszewski, and Edward Skeuse. An interesting sidelight of the 1936 season came about when sports scribes from the *Setonian* made their own attempt to create a distinctive nickname for the Seton Hall five to supersede the Pirates. They came up with the "Kerryblues" (the "Kerry" is a "bluish furred dog noted for its fighting instincts," and "blues," the school color), but this particular moniker never stuck. (SHU Archives.)

THE 1936–1937 TEAM. This squad earned a 5-10 record on the season. Pictured, from left to right, are the following: (front row) Morg Kelley, Pete Finnerty, Bob Madden, Jim Reynolds, Ed McNally (co-captain), Harry Purcell, Tony Zaycek, and Pete Leone; (back row) Warren Maurer, Frank Onorato, Jack Harrison, Bernie Coyle, Dick De Losa (co-captain), John Russell (head coach), Ed Sadowski, Jack McNally, Danny Lafelice, and Nick Parpin. Jim Reynolds, a star on this team, noted, "Coach Russell had good ball players and was a breath of fresh air. [He was] happy to be at the start of the upward turn in the program's fortunes" during the late 1930s. (SHU Archives.)

Hoops Scrum. Several road games and off-campus home games played in Newark were contested between 1935 and 1939 due to various scheduling problems. This particular contest was played before nearly 1,000 fans at the Orange Armory court on January 22, 1937, as Seton Hall defeated their rival from Jersey City, the Peacocks of St. Peter's College 30-23. The level of sportsmanship displayed was at its highest peak, and referee Tim Brenna reflected this fact in a letter reproduced in the *Setonian* on February 8, 1937: "He claims that our lads reflect smart coaching in their gentlemanly manners on the court." (SHU Archives.)

Flip Shot. This action photograph was taken at the Orange Armory as Seton Hall played and defeated Providence College 44-35 on the evening of March 6, 1937. Even though this was a down season for the Pirates, it was the second year in which athletic scholarships were offered to promising players. By the early 1930s, star performers who played at least 120 minutes and showed sportsmanship during the course of a season were awarded a large monogrammed S and certificate declaring the individual's right to wear that letter. In 1938, the first National Invitational Tournament was held in New York City, but Seton Hall did not qualify for this championship until three years later. (SHU Archives.)

COURT COUNCIL. Coach Russell (center) lectures players (from left to right) Bernard Coyle, Peter Leone, Jim Reynolds (captain), and Peter "Madame X" Finnerty in 1939. Among this group, Finnerty went on to play four years of baseball before joining the Seton Hall Athletic Hall of Fame in 1976. Russell compared the 1939 squad to that of 1909 and 1919 through the following analogy: "In the olden days there was a maximum of brains and a minimum of speed. . . . Today it is a maximum of speed and a minimum of brains. Speed and more speed is the keynote today." The 1938–1939 team went 15-7 on the season, but a singular win on March 3, 1939, against Scranton 52-39 marked the beginning of a 41-game unbeaten string. (SHU Archives.)

THE HI-S CLUB. Formed in 1938 by coach Russell, the Hi-S Club was made up of players from the team and served not only as a booster club but to help secure amenities for the team. This included signing petitions for a trainer and training table along with the purchase of sweaters through sponsorship of a dance and raffle. From left to right are the following: (front row) Bernard Coyle, Peter Leone, H. David Purcell (vice president), Frank Delaney, and Frank Onorato; (middle row) Peter F.X. Finnerty (secretary), James E. Reynolds (president), and William Thomas (treasurer); (back row) Nick Parpan, Charles Judge, and Edward Ryan. Not pictured is Fr. Charles E. Lillis (moderator), who also served as director of athletics at Seton Hall from 1927 to 1945. (SHU Archives.)

BLOCK OUT. A Seton Hall player goes up for the rejection as Ed Sadowski (No. 11) waits underneath the basket in anticipation of a rebound in this 1939 contest. The 1938–1939 squad went on an ironman tour in which they beat four teams (Ithaca College 36-35, Colgate 45-43, Hobart College 46-40, and St. Bonaventure 49-41) in four days between January 18 and 21, all on the road! The lineup included Bernard Coyle, Frank Delaney, Peter Finnerty, Charles Judge (manager), Peter Leone, Frank Onorato, Nick Parpan, Harry Purcell, Jim Reynolds, Edward Ryan, and Ed Sadowski. (SHU Archives.)

ED SADOWSKI. Standing at six feet five inches tall and weighing 265 pounds, Ed Sadowski, also known as "Big Ed," was credited by coach Russell for helping to put Seton Hall on the basketball map. The Akron, Ohio native also went by the term "One Man Gang," as shown in a 1939 game against Hobart in which he fractured his hand but still managed to score 29 points. He followed this up with 24 points against St. Bonaventure the following evening. Sadowski scored 757 points over the course of his Seton Hall career en route to selection on the 1938–1939 All-East Team and All-American consideration by 1940. He also played in the College All-Star game in Chicago during the 1941 season and became the first Seton Hall alumnus to play in the Basketball Association of America (BAA). Sadowski suited up for various teams, including the Fort Wayne Zollners, Detroit Eagles, and Toronto Huskies, before reuniting with coach Russell in Boston as a member of the Celtics a year later. He was a First Team All-BBA in 1947–1948 before earning entry to the Seton Hall Athletic Hall of Fame in 1974. (SHU Archives.)

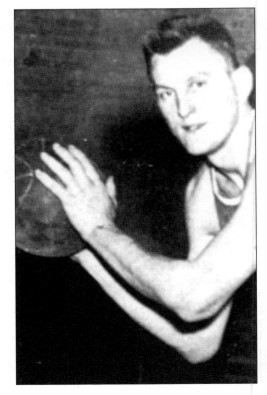

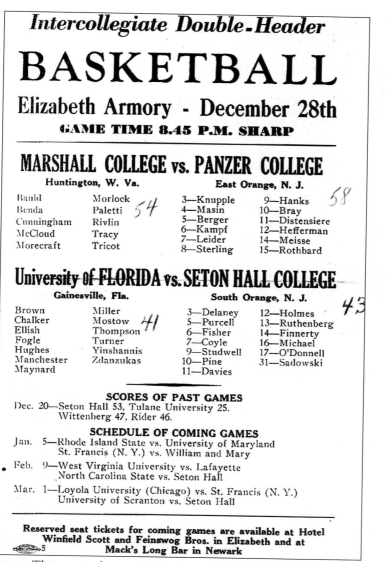

Intercollegiate Double-Header

BASKETBALL

Elizabeth Armory - December 28th

GAME TIME 8.45 P.M. SHARP

MARSHALL COLLEGE vs. PANZER COLLEGE

Huntington, W. Va.		East Orange, N. J.	
Bauld	Morlock	3—Knupple	9—Hanks
Benda	Paletti	4—Masin	10—Bray
Cunningham	Rivlin	5—Berger	11—Distensiere
McCloud	Tracy	6—Kampf	12—Hefferman
Morecraft	Tricot	7—Leider	14—Meisse
		8—Sterling	15—Rothbard

54 *58*

University of FLORIDA vs. SETON HALL COLLEGE

Gainesville, Fla.		South Orange, N. J.	
Brown	Miller	3—Delaney	12—Holmes
Chalker	Mostow	5—Purcell	13—Ruthenberg
Ellish	Thompson	6—Fisher	14—Finnerty
Fogle	Turner	7—Coyle	16—Michael
Hughes	Yinshannis	9—Studwell	17—O'Donnell
Manchester	Zdanzukas	10—Pine	31—Sadowski
Maynard		11—Davies	

41 *43*

SCORES OF PAST GAMES

Dec. 20—Seton Hall 53, Tulane University 25.
Wittenberg 47, Rider 46.

SCHEDULE OF COMING GAMES

Jan. 5—Rhode Island State vs. University of Maryland
St. Francis (N. Y.) vs. William and Mary

Feb. 9—West Virginia University vs. Lafayette
North Carolina State vs. Seton Hall

Mar. 1—Loyola University (Chicago) vs. St. Francis (N. Y.)
University of Scranton vs. Seton Hall

**Reserved seat tickets for coming games are available at Hotel
Winfield Scott and Feinswog Bros. in Elizabeth and at
Mack's Long Bar in Newark**

INTERSECTIONAL. This typical promotional announcement shows a collegiate hoops doubleheader, which came into vogue during the early 1930s when promoter Ned Irish began a trend of scheduling east-against-west contests at Madison Square Garden. The Elizabeth Armory hosted this contest on December 28, 1939, and Seton Hall played the University of Florida, making it the Pirates's second game against a team from the Deep South (the first was played and won eight days earlier against Tulane 53-25) and first opposite a representative of the modern-day Southeastern Conference. Seton Hall defeated the Gators 43-41. In terms of visionary match-ups, the following newspaper account from the early 1940s looks into the proverbial crystal ball: "Father Charles Lillis [athletic director] . . . enthused by the reception accorded the teams, made plans to contact western collegiate teams to come to Newark . . . at the 113th Infantry Regiment Armory. 'I am convinced that Newark and the suburban territory will support big time college basketball,' said Father Lillis. 'If possible we will attempt to bring teams like Notre Dame, Indiana, Purdue, Villanova and Georgetown to meet Setonia. I am certain that the games will win support.'" (SHU Archives.)

GOAL LINE. Pirate player Frank Delaney (No. 6) puts up a shot during an early-season game in 1939 before a tightly knotted group of spectators to the extreme left and a pushy defender immediately in front of him. Among the possible witnesses was a young basketball coach from nearby St. Cecilia's High School who attended classes at Seton Hall to sharpen his teaching skills. This individual led the Saints to a 10-9 record during the 1939–1940 season in his first job in athletics, but Vince Lombardi abandoned basketball and attained greater fame as a football coach. (SHU Archives.)

PERFECTION! The second undefeated team in school history was the 1939–1940 team (the 1910–1911, 4-0 season was the first), which went 19-0. Pictured, from left to right, are the following: (front row) Ed Ryan, Pete Finnerty, Bob Davies, Harry Purcell, Bobby Fisher, Vinnie Michael, Frank Delany, and Bernie Coyle; (back row) John Russell (head coach), Dr. Henry Turner (team physician), Bob Holm, Ray Studwell, John Ruthenberg, Ed Sadowski, Kenny Pine, Connie O'Donnell, Nick Parpan, and Bill Thomas (manager). In 1939, the school spent $4,250.02 on the basketball program but earned only $80.50 in return revenue. This changed in a few years, but Seton Hall also had altruistic impulses when it came to the spirit of gamesmanship. On February 9, 1940, the Pirates played Rider College in the first of a benefit series for the National Foundation for Infantile Paralysis (polio), which were contested annually through the mid-1950s. (SHU Archives.)

Two
THE GOLDEN AGE
1940–1950

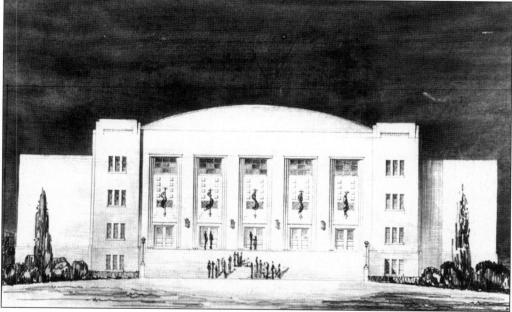

WALSH GYMNASIUM. This gray spot brick structure, dubbed the "million-dollar gym" due to the cost (which ranged from $600,000 to $800,000), was opened for basketball play during the winter of 1941. The centerpiece of these architectural plans included a basketball court measuring 50 by 90 feet, which could be divided for practice and regulation games simultaneously, made of a thick, non-warp, cross-grain surface, which was more durable than the traditional pine found in less up-to-date venues. The cantilever construction used is defined by a lack of external brackets, therefore allowing obstruction-free viewing by the 3,200 spectators who could fit into the grandstands. Msgr. James Kelley, college president, began project planning in 1935 by taking an 18-month tour to look at various college gymnasiums across America. He based the Walsh Gymnasium concept on facilities found at St. Catherine's College and Yale University for its multipurpose dynamics. The new building contained not only a basketball court but a movie theater, squash court, Ping-Pong table, fencing pitch, and two pools (one for swimming and another for hockey when refrigerated). (SHU Archives.)

THE CORNERSTONE. Thomas J. Walsh, archbishop of Newark, lays the ceremonial block at the dedication of the new gymnasium (which still bears his name) on June 29, 1939, before more than 500 onlookers, including Msgr. James Kelley and William A. Griffin, auxiliary bishop. This new structure was partially located in South Orange and Newark but became a prominent part of the Seton Hall campus. Monsignor Kelley was responsible for filling the interior cavity of the cornerstone, which included such items as copies of the college catalog, *Setonian*, and 75th anniversary history book. The cornerstone is not to be opened until 2139. (SHU Archives.)

BOX SEAT. Archbishop Walsh headed the Archdiocese of Newark from 1928 to 1952. He was an athlete and sports fan who played baseball with famed New York Giants manager John McGraw during his undergraduate days at St. Bonaventure College. He later initiated a public program to build the new gymnasium by February 1935 with the target goal of $250,000, which he opened with a personal donation of $1,000. Here, Archbishop Walsh leaves Walsh Gymnasium after a 1941 contest. (SHU Archives.)

STRIKE UP THE BAND. The Seton Hall College Musical Band (founded in 1936) performed during basketball games and at victory rallies. The original ensemble was augmented with a special drum and bugle corps, which brought membership up to 60, as evidenced in this 1941 photograph. Their most memorable numbers included the Seton Hall standards "Alma Mater" and "White and Blue." Variations on the band concept appeared at various times in school history, with the latest being the pep band that still plays at both men's and women's contests. Among the most memorable groups to make music was a tavern troupe hired during the 1960s that knew the words to only "On Wisconsin" and the "Notre Dame Fight Song." (SHU Archives.)

A SIDELINE VIEW. A pensive coach Russell surrounded by assistant coaches, players, and fans look toward the court in 1941 as they watch their Pirates. Five years earlier, a *Setonian* reporter named Tom Duggan wrote about the finer points of spectating in his article entitled "How to Watch a Basketball Game." Duggan wrote, "When attending a basketball game, always take a friend. This will double the gate receipts and at the same time will provide conversation between the halves. In addition to the friend, bring some sort of noise-making device, if possible a cannon, at least a bass drum. When the home team is winning, raise considerable cain with this noise provider, if the team is losing sit glumly by and sulk. Cheering now and then helps to pep up a team, especially when the cheerers do their job proficiently. When cheering, open the mouth wide." (SHU Archives.)

BOB DAVIES, ALL-AMERICAN. Journalist Sid Dorfman called Bob Davies the "local Michael Jordan." Standing six feet one inch tall, Davies was known as the "Harrisburg Houdini," "Blonde Bomber," "Silver Whippet," and "Li'l Abner" or "Abbie" (due to his resemblance to the cartoon character) among others. Davies was elected team captain twice, the team's most valuable player (MVP) three times, and college All-Star Game MVP in 1942. He also became Seton Hall's first All-American player who won the honor in 1941 and 1942. He was a well-rounded campus figure who joined the Order of Cross and Crescent (the honor society), the Rifle Club, and the French Club. Davies played four years of baseball, arguably his best sport, which the Boston Red Sox scouts recognized when they offered him a minor league contract. He served as an inspiration for the 25-volume Chip Hilton sports literature series, by Long Island University basketball coach Clair Bee, who was wowed by Davies's performance in the 1941 NIT. Davies's No. 11 was retired in 1950, and he became a charter member of the Seton Hall Athletic Hall of Fame in 1973. (SHU Archives.)

THE BLONDE BOMBER. Newspaper writer David Eisenberg had an observation about Bob Davies after Seton Hall's victory over Rhode Island State College in the 1941 NIT: "Halley's Comet has a rival today, Bob Davies is the new satellite, and the firmament across which he blazes in brilliant hue, is a basketball court." Davies went on to play professional basketball with the Brooklyn Indians of the American Basketball League in 1943–1944 and Rochester Royals from 1945 to 1955. He was an eight-time National Basketball League (NBL) and NBA All-Star, NBL most valuable player in 1947, and the first professional to have 20 assists in a game. He was inducted into the Naismith Memorial Basketball Hall of Fame in 1970, the same year *Sport Magazine* named him the sixth greatest player of the first half of the 20th century. (SHU Archives.)

THE INNOVATOR. Various historians of the game believed that Bob Cousy was the second coming of Bob Davies. Davies was a prototype of the modern forward who learned his unique behind the back dribble while watching Stanford All-American Hank Luisetti in the 1938 movie *Campus Confessions* and by studying his technique in magazines. Once asked how to stop Davies, Clair Bee brought up the idea of using handcuffs and stated, "I wish he were on my team. I wish I had five like him, as a matter of fact." Honey Russell noted that Davies was the "greatest play maker I've ever coached or seen play in college or pro basketball. He's a likeable boy, a good student, a fine kid to teach and one who listens—and absorbs." (SHU Archives.)

TRAILBLAZERS. The first Seton Hall team to earn prime-time status was the 1940–1941 squad, which also became the earliest Pirate five to visit Madison Square Garden and make it to postseason play. The team earned a bid to the NIT, which was more prestigious than the NCAA Tournament during the 1940s. A first-round victory over Rhode Island State 70-54 was played before a Garden crowd of 18,341, a record at that time. Davies had 19 points, but that was the last in a streak of 41 straight wins. The Pirates finished with a 20-2 record for the year and were named New Jersey's Best Athletic Team for 1941 by the Associated Press in a unanimous vote. The team is pictured here, from left to right, as follows: (front row) Bob Holm, Bob Fisher, Ken Pine, John Ruthenberg, Bob Davies, Al Negretti, and Edward Ryan; (middle row) Ray Studwell, Bob Pine, Nick Parpan, Ben Scharnus, George Poeltler, and Vincent Michaels; (back row) James Kerwin (assistant manager), Gerald Dalton (assistant manager), Frank Delaney, Douglas King, Bob Behan, and Frank Faas (manager). (SHU Archives.)

THE "WONDER FIVE." This mural by Louis Raggi depicts, from left to right, Ken Pine, John Ruthenberg, Bob Fisher, coach Russell, Bob Holm, and Bob Davies. It is located in the lobby of Walsh Gymnasium. The oil painting appeared *c.* 1942 and was considered the first of it kind to honor current players. *Newark Star-Ledger* columnist Jim Ogle wrote about this particular item in a 1942-era column, "The artist did a masterful job in catching the mood of the various players. Davies [is] in his traditional slouch. . . . Holm is there with his hands on his hips. . . . Russell is shown in practice clothes. . . . Fisher has that ever present funny grin. . . . Ruthenberg is his usual somber self. . . . Pine . . . reminds one of Danny Kaye." (Courtesy of SHU Sports Information.)

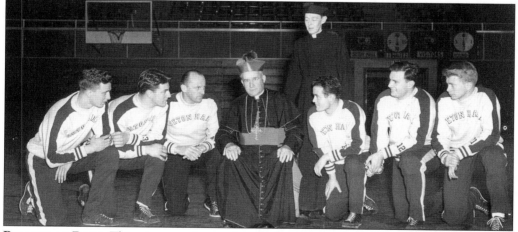

PIRATES AT PRAY. This picture, taken on March 8, 1941, on the court of Walsh Gymnasium, includes Archbishop Thomas J. Walsh, Fr. Charles Lillis (athletic director), Bob Davies, Bob Fisher, Bob Holm, Ken Pine, John Ruthenberg, and coach Russell. Fisher was termed the "Flatbush Flurry" since he hailed from Brooklyn, and Pine, the center, was an All–New York football, basketball, and baseball selection in 1938 before taking the mound as a pitcher on the Seton Hall nine. Holm (nicknamed "Turnips"), who used to stick a wad of gum in the supporting stanchion of the basket before each game for good luck, was the nephew of famed swimmer and Pirate booster Eleanor Holm. Holm won a gold medal at the 1932 Olympics but was dismissed from the 1936 team for drinking champagne on the trip over to Berlin. Collectively, the team went 55-5 as a varsity unit (14-1 as freshmen) between 1939 and 1942, and the Wonder Five were ultimately elected to the Seton Hall University Athletic Hall of Fame at various times between 1973 and 1989. (SHU Archives.)

FETE FOR THE FEAT! This montage shows how residents of South Orange, along with Seton Hall students, administrators, and friends of the college, celebrated the Pirates and their NIT appearance in March 1941. The local press observed *c.* 1940, "So far as the picturesque college in South Orange, New Jersey, is concerned, basketball certainly has out-distanced all other sports." Jim Durkin, sports publicity director at the time, stated, "The game is to Seton Hall, now what football is to Notre Dame." (SHU Archives.)

TIP DRILL. Coach Russell was a firm believer in stressing the fundamentals during practice sessions. This early 1940s look shows George Poeltler grab a rebound over his teammates in a scrimmage game. During the early 1940s, Russell also conducted coaching clinics at Walsh Gymnasium with his friends Nat Holman of the City College of New York (CCNY) and Ed Kelleher of Fordham University. This preparation paid off during the 1941–1942 campaign, as Seton Hall earned a number of memorable wins. Among the memorable close calls was a 43-42 loss to a Dartmouth team, which went on to the NCAA Championship game against Stanford that year before a standing-room-only crowd of 6,100 at Walsh Gymnasium. (SHU Archives.)

THE LAUNCHING PAD. Seton Hall became a regional athletic obsession during the early 1940s, as shown by a vying war for the Pirates made by various venues across the region. After successful engagements at their new home court and various sites in Newark, Seton Hall found a second home in other major cities along the eastern seaboard. Seton Hall has played several road games at the legendary Philadelphia Palestra (built in 1927) and New York City's Madison Square Garden, where the Pirates were the marquee team in a number of doubleheaders and tournament tilts. (SHU Archives.)

THE 1941–1942 TEAM. This group posted a 16-3 record and was the swan song for the Wonder Five, each of whom received gold wristwatches after their last game together on March 3, 1942, against LaSalle College. World War II soon caused a manpower depletion in athletic teams across the nation and, as a result, freshmen were allowed to compete with the varsity squad during this time of transition. Here, coach Russell explains the concepts of ball control to younger members of his team. From left to right are Al Diehl, Russ Regan, Ed McLaughlin, Russell, Kevin Connors, Al Negretti, and Doug King. Negretti went on to play professional basketball with the Washington Capitals of the BAA and entered the Seton Hall Athletic Hall of Fame in 1997. (SHU Archives.)

KEVIN "CHUCK" CONNORS. Before attaining widespread repute as the "Rifleman" of television fame, Kevin "Chuck" Connors was a student at Seton Hall from 1941 to 1942. He was a center on Russell's freshmen squad that season before moving up to the varsity, where he averaged between two and six points per contest. Connors weighed 25 different scholarship offers before coming to South Orange, and as he noted in a late 1950s interview, "I was in college to get an education and never lost sight of that. . . . I didn't want any of those snap courses. . . . So I persuaded the priests there to let me study literature and philosophy." Connors also played professional baseball with the Brooklyn Dodgers and Chicago Cubs after the war, but another claim to fame occurred when he became the first professional player to smash a glass backboard, which he did in pregame warm-ups before the Boston Celtics inaugural game on November 5, 1946. (SHU Archives.)

JOHN RUTHENBERG. John Ruthenberg was a charter member of the Wonder Five who stood six feet two inches tall and was better known to his fans as "Big John." He was a native of Akron, Ohio, before coming to Seton Hall, where he graduated in 1942. Prior to earning a diploma, Ruthenberg was not only a four-year starter on the basketball team but also played baseball and belonged to the Parking Committee, the Knights of Setonia, and served as vice president of the Physical Education Club. He joined the U.S. Army Air Corps in 1942 and was killed in action when his plane was shot down over Germany. In tribute to his heroism, Ruthenberg was honored during a dedication ceremony (featuring actor Pat O'Brien, who gained cinematic fame portraying "Knute Rockne, All-American"), where his name was affixed to the first building of the Veterans' Village Barracks complex, constructed for use by military veterans who attended Seton Hall on the G.I. Bill of Rights. Ruthenberg was posthumously named to the Seton Hall Athletic Hall of Fame in 1997. (SHU Archives.)

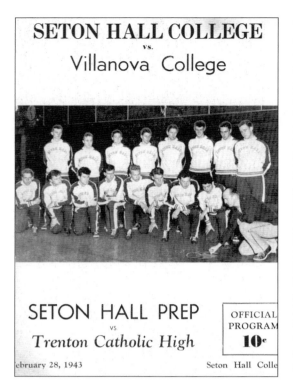

SETON HALL COLLEGE
vs.
Villanova College

SETON HALL PREP
vs.
Trenton Catholic High

OFFICIAL
PROGRAM
10¢

ebruary 28, 1943   Seton Hall Colle

WARTIME BALL. Between 1941 and 1943, the Pirates had a combined 32-5 record in which they played not only their usual regional rivals but also military base teams, including the Army Air Corps (Turner Field, Georgia) and the U.S. Coast Guard (Brooklyn Battalion) in 1942. The 1942 squad, pictured here from left to right, included the following: (front row) Frank Saul, Frank Bellack, John Finnegan, Bob Doyle, John Macknowski, Tom Larkin, John McCarron, Al Dente, and coach Russell; (back row) Ed McLaughlin, Doug King, Lou Toia, Dick Birdsall, Tom Byrnes, Bob Fitzgerald, Al Diehl, and Al Negretti. Other Seton Hall players joined the professional ranks, such as Ben Scharnus, who played for the Cleveland Rebels and Providence Steamrollers. In addition, Byrnes played with the Baltimore Bullets, Indianapolis Jets, Tri-Cities Blackhawks, and New York Knicks while Fitzgerald and McCarron both suited up for the Toronto Huskies during the late 1940s. (SHU Archives.)

ON THE HOME FRONT. With freshmen eligibility rules relaxed during the mid-1940s, these young players were part of Russell's final team during his first tour of duty at Seton Hall in 1943. Pictured, from left to right, are Dick Birdsall, Tom Burns, Tom Larkin, Bob Doyle, and Frank Bellack. The 1942–1943 team went 16-2 on the season and defeated Niagara 33-26, Cornell 29-28, Bradley Tech 40-36, the College of the Holy Cross 45-30, Providence College 47-38, Yale 43-32, and the American Institute 71-38 among others. (SHU Archives.)

THE WINTER OF 1944. During the 1944 campaign, defensive goaltending (subsequently known as the the Mikan Rule) was outlawed after George Mikan, the six-foot seven-inch DePaul center, and his dominating play made for an unfair advantage. Another rule change came when five (instead of the four in effect since 1910) personal fouls disqualified a player and unlimited substitutions were made legal. Seton Hall hosted a junior varsity schedule during the 1945–1946 season under head coach Harry Singleton, and the team subsequently went 16-8, beating such teams as the New York Maritime Academy 61-45, Bergstrom AAF 45-24, and Tilton Hospital 57-34. (SHU Archives.)

A GAME GRAPPLE. Action during the mid-1940s shows Pirate players battling for the ball. The Seton Hall freshmen team was coached by Harry Singleton in 1945–1946 as they played an impromptu schedule such as Bainbridge Naval Training, Brooklyn Cathedral, Rider College Junior Varsity, and Manhattan College. The Seton Hall roster included John Connelly, Frank Gormely, Bob Kennedy, Sean Brady, William Fay, and William Black. Ironically, Seton Hall beat Honey Russell's Manhattan College Jaspers 56-29 in February 1946. That same year, Seton Hall was admitted to the NCAA and Metropolitan Intercollegiate Athletic Association. (SHU Archives.)

HOMECOMING. This photograph shows the front of Walsh Gymnasium at its peak in 1947. School enrollment rose from 142 to 902 in 1945 (and 3,000 by 1947) precipitated by the G.I. Bill of Rights, which provided a tuition-free college education for returning servicemen. Seton Hall benefited as enrollment rose 95 percent over pre-1945 figures, making it the highest rate in the nation. These new Pirate fans could purchase a seat in the bleachers for the student rate of 90¢. The gym at this time seated 2,995 but could expand upwards of 3,400 as circumstances warranted. Included were special exhibition matches featuring the Rochester Royals during the late 1940s. (SHU Archives.)

JAMES F. KELLEY. The president of Seton Hall from 1936 to 1949, Msgr. James F. Kelley was the individual primarily responsible for bringing Seton Hall into the mainstream of collegiate athletics while maintaining a high level of academic attainment among the student body. Kelley was 34 years old when appointed the chief executive of Seton Hall and was the youngest college president in the entire nation at that time. Seton Hall had 281 students between 1926 and 1933, and by the time Monsignor Kelley left in 1949, that number had swelled to over 4,000, due in part to the fame brought about by a successful athletic program. Honey Russell was hired by Kelley during the late 1930s. Although Seton Hall could not field a football team of Notre Dame caliber, the construction of Walsh Gymnasium became the Pirates' proverbial lightning rod. Monsignor Kelley was elected to the Seton Hall Athletic Hall of Fame in 1975. (SHU Archives.)

COACH DAVIES. Bob Davies was named head coach on March 15, 1946, making him one of the youngest in the country at the time. Davies compiled a 24-3 record in 1946–1947, a feat made all the more impressive considering that he also coached the baseball team to a 26-6 record that spring and played basketball in Rochester, New York, in between. Davies left South Orange after one season when he received a substantial contract to play for the Royals full-time and continue his graduate studies at Columbia University in the off season. Pictured, from left to right, are Frank Saul, Bobby Wanzer, Davies, and John Macknowski. Saul, Wanzer, and Davies each played in the first documented professional exhibition game at Walsh Gymnasium for the Rochester Royals against the Indianapolis Kautsky on October 29, 1947. They also played together on the 1951 NBA Championship Royals. (SHU Archives.)

THE 1947–1948 TEAM. This squad went 18-4 on the year under the guidance of head coach Jack Reitemeier and recorded eight straight wins to start the season. Pictured, from left to right, are as follows: (first row) Howie Janotta, Frank Saul, Bobby Wanzer, Tom Mullins, and John Macknowski; (second row) Jack Reitemeier (head coach), Bob "Bo" Hartmann, Dick Hammock, Harry Renner, and Mick Richel (student manager); (third row) Richard Nagle, John Nuszer, Walter Kostyshyn, John McDermott, and Tom Gibbons; (fourth row) Thomas LeVerte, Dick Honeker, James Kelly, and John Reilly. (Team members Paul Mansberry and Tony Sisti are not pictured.) (SHU Archives.)

JACK REITEMEIER. Reitemeier posted a 34-12 record as the basketball coach at Seton Hall College from 1947 to 1949. Reitemeier (who bears a striking resemblance to Huey P. Long) was a graduate of Purdue University, where he played basketball, football, and golf, and was a contemporary of fellow Boilermaker and basketball strategist John Wooden. Reitemeier headed the Seton Hall Preparatory School program from 1938 to 1942, where he amassed a cumulative record of 100-6. In between coaching, he served as a physical education instructor and business manager at Seton Hall College during the early and mid-1940s. During World War II, he served in the navy and became chief aid to Gene Tunney (former heavyweight boxing champion), who ran a physical fitness program for his fellow sailors. (SHU Archives.)

"PEP." Frank Benjamin Saul, known better as "Pep," earned a bachelor of science degree in 1949. Saul's initial impression of Seton Hall's basketball program included the view that the Pirates were "very team oriented and we had a winning attitude. I always felt our scrimmages were tougher than most of our games because we were such a good squad." As a student at Seton Hall, he belonged to the Knights of Setonia, played baseball in between starring on the 1942–1943 team, and earned captaincy of the 1946 through 1949 hoop squads. Saul was the first 1,000-point career scorer in Seton Hall history and ended up with 1,011 total. He was elected to the Seton Hall Athletic Hall of Fame in 1973, and his No. 3 jersey is permanently retired. (SHU Archives.)

BLUE SKIES. The Seton Hall–Holy Cross game on February 8, 1947, was counted among the most memorable close calls in program history as the Pirates lost to the Crusaders 44-43. More than 2,800 ticket requests were turned down for this game, which was sold out since mid-January. Pep Saul (in the foreground) reaches for the ball over All-American George Kaftan (in the background) of Holy Cross. Under the guidance of Alvin "Doggie" Julian, the Crusaders fielded a team of five starters who all hailed from New York City. A young Bob Cousy came off the bench to contribute to the Holy Cross cause. The historical what-if postscript to this game came when Seton Hall rejected all postseason invitations in 1947 and Holy Cross went on to become the first eastern and Catholic college ever to win an NCAA title. (SHU Archives.)

THE COURT QUARTERBACK. Seton Hall star Pep Saul takes off downcourt as he smiles for the camera. He led the Pirates in scoring for three straight years with annual totals of 301, 304, and 319, respectively, between 1946 and 1949. He later became the first Seton Hall player of the post–World War II era to be picked in the NBA draft when he joined the Rochester Royals in 1949. Saul went on to win a title with the Royals in 1951 and earned three more between 1952 and 1954, when he joined George Mikan and the Minneapolis Lakers before ending his career with Baltimore and Milwaukee. (SHU Archives.)

BOBBY WANZER. A star player for the Pirates during the 1942–1943 and 1946–1947 seasons, Bobby Wanzer averaged 11.6 points per game on the 1946–1947 squad. Wanzer played for Bob Davies at Seton Hall and with him as a member of the Rochester Royals. They also share the distinction of having both played basketball with famed Cleveland Browns quarterback Otto Graham, a member of the Professional Football Hall of Fame. Davies was a teammate of Graham in 1945 as a member of the Royals and Wanzer at Colgate, where they played together on the Red Raider varsity as part of the V-12 Marines program during the 1943–1944 season. During the late 1940s, Wanzer joined the professional ranks with the Royals, where he averaged 11.7 points per game and was a five-time All-Star selection over his 10-year career. In 1952, he made history as the first professional player to hit over 90 percent of his free throw attempts in a season. Wanzer became a player-coach for the Royals from 1955 to 1958, and he guided the West squad in the 1958 NBA All-Star game. He was elected to the Seton Hall Athletic Hall of Fame in 1974 and the Naismith Memorial Basketball Hall of Fame in 1987 along with having his No. 8 jersey permanently retired by the school. (SHU Archives.)

DICK HAMMOCK. Born in Jersey City, Dick Hammock was a star player for the Seton Hall five from 1946 to 1949. Hammock was a co-captain of the 1947–1948 team and averaged five points per game during the 1948–1949 season. After graduation from Seton Hall Preparatory School, Hammock played a season at St. Bonaventure College and served in the military during World War II. The 1948 Seton Hall media guide featured the following piece on Hammock and his value to the team: "The comedian of the squad. Always keeps his mates in good humor with his wisecracks. Is serious on the court and is a good defensive performer. Held down a regular position last season. . . . His height off the boards makes him very important in a clutch." (SHU Archives.)

JOHN MACKNOWSKI. Known as "Whitey" (due to the hue of his hair), John Macknowski played for Seton Hall College from 1946 to 1948. Macknowski was a product of Lincoln High School in Jersey City prior to joining the freshman team at Seton Hall during the 1941–1942 season. He joined the varsity after serving in the navy for three years during World War II. The play of Macknowski, who averaged 11 points per game during the 1947–1948 season, was recounted by Jim Ogle of the *Newark Star-Ledger,* who wrote in the late 1940s, "He is a set shot artist and a dangerous shot whenever he gets his hands on the ball. He is also a good floorman." He played for the Syracuse Nationals from 1948 to 1952 before his election to the Seton Hall Athletic Hall of Fame in 1975. (SHU Archives.)

UNDERHANDED. Seton Hall star Dave Latimer (No. 22) takes a "bang zoom to the moon" move in order to elude a Terrier defender as the Pirates tangled with St. Francis in this February 4, 1949 road contest. Under second-year coach Jack Reitemeier, Seton Hall went 16-8, which came in the wake of an even more successful 1947–1948 campaign in which the Pirates went 18-4. During the 1948–1949 season, the Pirates did not fall below 53 points for any single contest over such schools as Detroit 55-43, the College of William and Mary 59-55, Texas A & M 69-55, Lafayette 56-47, and Albright 68-48. (SHU Archives.)

LEADER OF THE PACK. Here is a takeaway by Harry "Stretch" Renner (No. 11), who orchestrates a fast break upcourt against the Blackbirds of Long Island University on February 17, 1949. This game featured indications of rule changes that came into effect during the 1948–1949 season, including the requirement that all backboards be made of glass and coaches were now allowed to converse with players during time-outs. Included on the 1948–1949 roster were Walter Ciborowski, Tom Gibbons, Richard Hammock, Bob "Bo" Hartmann (co-captain), Howard Janotta, George Keefe, Walt Kostyshyn, Sam Lackaye, Dave Latimer, Thomas LeVerte, Dave Putnam, Harry "Stretch" Renner, John Reilly, Frank Saul, and Louis Varous. Along with Saul, the other player from this squad to join him in the NBA was Howie Janotta. Ironically, Janotta transferred to Seton Hall from Long Island University after World War II and scored 208 points in 1948–1949, which helped land him a place on the Baltimore Bullets a year later. (SHU Archives.)

REJECTION. This photograph shows David Putnam (No. 21) and Dave Latimer (No. 22) vying for a rebound against Texas Wesleyan on January 22, 1949. The influence of the American Southwest gripped certain segments of the Seton Hall population as a local newspaper recounted how some students joined the Fort Worth–based five en route to the game. "Four enterprising youngsters obtained 10-gallon hats, recalling that Texas Wesleyan last season wore sombreros as they did during their present visit here. They mingled with the Texans as they entered the gym and passed without challenge. P.S.—Their allegiance to Texas Wesleyan ended as soon as the game began." (SHU Archives.)

FREE THROW FRENZY. Pirate center Thomas LeVerte lets one fly from the charity stripe against the Creighton Blue Jays as Seton Hall players jockey for position to take possession in case of a misfire. The Pirates won this March 6, 1947 contest 62-47. LeVerte, a transfer student from West Virginia University who stared for the Mountaineer NIT team in 1945–1946, sat out the requisite season prior to starring for Seton Hall from 1947 to 1949. The Creighton game also featured a program milestone as "Pep" Saul scored the 1,000th point of his career and became the first Pirate player ever to accomplish this feat. (SHU Archives.)

EDWARD "TED" HUSING. Husing's signature line, "Good afternoon, everyone, everywhere," became a national byword during the 1930s and 1940s. Husing (known as "Mr. Radio Football") is shown talking with fellow Seton Hall adherent Harry Nash, sports director of WNJR in Newark during the 1947–1948 season. A sportscaster for the Columbia Broadcasting System (CBS) for 18 years (and later with the Mutual Radio Network), Husing called not only college football but also tennis, crew regattas, and the Kentucky Derby. His mellifluous baritone, vast vocabulary, and command of timing also served him as the host of "Ted Husing's Bandstand," a musical program on New York City radio station WHN. (SHU Archives.)

HOLD THE PRESSES! Ted Husing visited Seton Hall as a guest of honor for the Night of Stars celebration held on December 27, 1947, in order to formally dedicate the new press box (named in his honor) located in Walsh Gymnasium. After the festivities ended, Seton Hall defeated Rutgers 46-43 in the first documented television basketball broadcast in school history. The Pirates appeared on WNEW of New York City. College radio station WSOU FM (the first college FM radio station in New Jersey), also quartered in Walsh Gymnasium, went on the air on April 14, 1948, and one of their first program staples was Seton Hall University and Preparatory School Basketball. (SHU Archives.)

54

MARTY GLICKMAN. The legendary Marty Glickman was the first man to popularize basketball broadcasting. He coined the term "swish" and made "top of the key" and "baseline" part of the modern basketball lexicon. Glickman called several college basketball contests from Madison Square Garden on station WMGM during the late 1940s and early 1950s. He also pioneered the field of sports radio as host of a talk show on WHN during the late 1940s prior to calling games for the Knicks, Jets, and football Giants during his five-decade career. Prior to stepping behind the microphone, Glickman was an athlete at Syracuse University, where he ran track. He later became a friend to Seton Hall, as shown here, where he talks to various WSOU staffers in 1950. Glickman not only announced various Seton Hall games at the Garden (including newsreel narration for the 1953 NIT Championship game), but also served as play-by-play voice of the Pirates on WNEW radio from 1986 to 1988. His influence can be found in scores of other broadcasters connected to Seton Hall, including Harry Nash, Bill Moore, "Uncle Fred" Sayles, Spencer Ross, Bob Ley '76 (ESPN commentator), Jim Hunter '82 (Baltimore Orioles announcer), and others. (SHU Archives.)

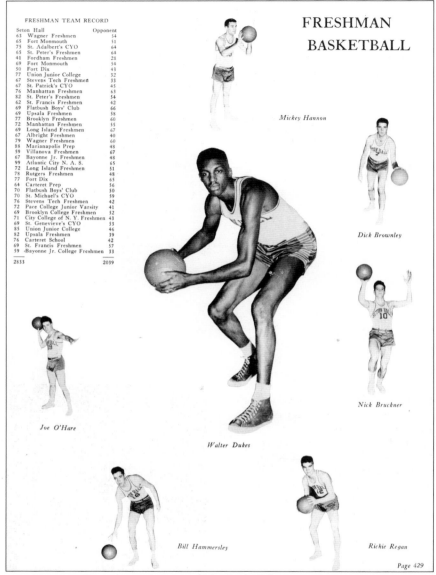

FRESHMAN BASKETBALL

Mickey Hannon

Dick Brownley

Nick Bruckner

Joe O'Hare

Walter Dukes

Bill Hammersley

Richie Regan

Page 429

FABULOUS FROSH. Throughout Seton Hall basketball history, the program featured freshmen and junior varsity teams that produced a host of future Pirate stars over the years. A rule in effect during the late 1940s and early 1950s that allowed for schools with an enrollment under 1,000 to place freshmen on the varsity did not apply to Seton Hall at this time, so these squads became a prime training ground for budding varsity stars. Among the most important individuals affiliated with basketball talent development were John and Thomas A. Murphy. Both are members of the Seton Hall Athletic Hall of Fame; John was inducted 1989 and Thomas in 1974. Thomas served as a scout for 15 years under coaches Russell and Regan, while John coached the freshmen during the 1950s. Pictured is the 1949–1950 team, which later combined to lead the Seton Hall varsity to a 80-12 record between 1950 and 1953. With a 39-1 record, this aggregation was the top team of its level in the country that year by averaging 70.8 points per game against only 50.9 for their opposition. (SHU Archives.)

Three

THE GLORY YEARS
1950–1960

BLOCK DOWN. At midcentury, Seton Hall marked a milestone when they attained university status by act of the New Jersey state legislature on June 2, 1950. The basketball team took this new designation with them into prime-time competition. In this view, Seton Hall takes on Villanova and their All-American Paul Arizin, who is blocked out by Bobby Hurt of the Pirates. Dave Putnam (No. 21) and John Ligos (No. 4) look on. This 1950 contest was an early glimpse into what Seton Hall faced in Big East play three decades later against big name competition, superlative athletes, and a yearly home and away game against the same opponent. Arizin, who later played with his hometown Philadelphia Warriors, was limited to 16 points in the first half of this contest at Walsh Gymnasium, but in the return match at the Palestra, his 41 points were a record mark for the arena and city at that time. Even though Seton Hall lost both contests and ended the 1949–1950 season at 11-15, the return of coach Russell in the first year of his second tour of duty on the Pirate sidelines soon payed substantial dividends in the win column. (SHU Archives.)

AN AERIAL PASS. This jump pass from Sam Lackaye to Paul Latimer on the far corner helps break the Scarlet Knight press upcourt in this intrastate battle against Rutgers on February 6, 1950. Lackaye, nicknamed the "Golden Boy," started his collegiate career at Villanova with his fellow freshmen teammate Sherman White in 1948, but both eventually transferred to other institutions. Seton Hall featured Lackaye, while White gained fame and notoriety at Long Island University during the early 1950s. (SHU Archives.)

THE SWINGMAN. A precariously footed Sam Lackaye looks for help from his teammates in this 1950 match against Villanova. Among the top players in 1950 were team captain Bob "Bo" Hartmann (known for his defensive prowess) and a pair of 500-plus career scorers, Dave Latimer (501 from 1948 to 1951) and Roy Belliveau (652 between 1949 and 1952) who earned a place in the Seton Hall Athletic Hall of Fame in 1986. The 1949–1950 Pirates ended their season with four straight wins over Hawaii 80-69, Georgetown 77-65, Valparaiso 81-61, and St. Bonaventure 42-41 and entered the 1950–1951 year with four more over Rhode Island State 70-64, New York Athletic Club 58-46, LeMoyne 63-53, and St. Peter's 87-52. (SHU Archives.)

A Flying Fin. Seton Hall star Bobby Hurt, who averaged 8 points per game in 1950–1951 (and 11 the year before), goes up for a layup with a Boston College defender attempting to block the ball during this February 3, 1951 contest. The Pirates prevailed against the Eagles 67-53, but this was only one of four victories against the future Big East foes in the year. Seton Hall also defeated Syracuse 45-44, Rutgers 62-4, and Georgetown 82-78 in 1951. The round-ball vernacular in vogue among coaches and players during the early 1950s included "ball hawk" (ball recovery expert), "figure eight" (when five players move in such a pattern), and "slam bangers" (erratic, careless play). (SHU Archives.)

One on Five. A single Seton Hall player, Dave Latimer (No. 17), takes on the entire Texas Wesleyan five here in 1950 game action. Among the Pirate defenders who made this steal possible was John Ligos, who played in 81 games from 1949 to 1952. Ligos noted that the Pirate teams of the early 1950s featured "jump shooting, strong defense, and all very smart players." Seton Hall showed intelligence on the floor during the 1950–1951 season as the team went 24-7 en route to the school's second NIT bid after rejecting an invitation to the now defunct National Catholic Invitational Tournament. (SHU Archives.)

WALTER DUKES. Standing at 6 feet 11 inches tall and nicknamed "Treetop" or "Wally," Walter Dukes was one of the school's all-time greatest players. Born in Youngstown, Ohio, and raised in Rochester, New York, Dukes found his way to Seton Hall through the efforts of his mother and former All-American Bob Davies, who played in Rochester during the late 1940s. Once at Seton Hall, Dukes matured into an all-around student who belonged to the Business Club, Interracial Council, Philosophy Circle, Marketing Club, Insurance Club, and Spanish Club in between playing basketball from 1950 to 1953. Overall, Dukes scored 1,789 total points, seventh on the all-time Seton Hall list, and he also set an NCAA season record of 734 rebounds in 1953, a mark that lasted until 1991. Dukes had good flexibility despite his size and often drew fouls. His 1953 total of 140 free throws out of 196 (.714 percent) and career total of 933 showed his skill at the charity stripe. He is also among only seven players in NCAA Division I history to have a career 20 points and 20 rebounds per-game average. Selected an All-American in 1953, Dukes also won the Haggerty Award for top player in the Metropolitan area and was named MVP of the 1953 NIT tournament prior to his selection into the first Seton Hall Athletic Hall of Fame class of 1973. Dukes's No. 5 jersey has been permanently retired by Seton Hall. (SHU Archives.)

DUKES CLOSE UP. Upon finishing his playing career with Seton Hall, Dukes teamed up with the world-famous Harlem Globetrotters from 1954 to 1955 after receiving a bonus of 3,000 silver dollars from team owner Abe Saperstein. Even though Dukes was selected as the territorial draft choice of the New York Knickerbockers in the first round of the 1953 NBA draft, he did not join the team until 1956. Dukes lasted one season with the Knicks before playing on the Detroit Pistons and Minneapolis Lakers over his eight-year career, which included 10.4 points and 11.3 rebounding averages, earning him NBA All-Star recognition three times. (SHU Archives.)

"And he was THAT big . . ."

MILE HIGH. This is a look at the seemingly hand-rim level shot by Walter Dukes in a 1951 game at Madison Square Garden. Seton Hall played a number of games across the Hudson and was counted among the best programs in the country during the 1950–1951 and 1951–1952 seasons, in which they recorded 24-7 and 25-3 records, respectively. This period also included two successive NIT bids, including a defeat of Beloit 71-57 and North Carolina State 71-59 in the first two rounds before bowing to Brigham Young in the semifinals and a consolation game to St. John's in double overtime of the 1951 classic. A loss to Tom Gola (who many consider the greatest all-around player in basketball history) and the LaSalle Explorers occurred in the first round a year later. (SHU Archives.)

THE CHAMPIONSHIP GAME. During the 1952–1953 season, the Pirates recorded the program's first 30-plus-win season with a 31-2 mark. In the course of that campaign, the Seton Hall juggernaut claimed such victims as Memphis State, Western Kentucky, Loyola, Dayton, Xaiver, and Louisville during a 27-game winning streak and No. 1 national ranking, which lasted through late February. An NIT invitation followed, and Seton Hall defeated Niagara in the first round 79-74, and two nights later Manhattan fell 76-58, resulting in a championship game match-up with ancient rival St. John's. Televised to the tri-state area by Channel 11, WPIX New York, viewers on Saturday, March 14, 1953, at 9:30 p.m. saw Seton Hall take their first lead three minutes into the game and were able to continue this momentum against the Redmen as Seton Hall won its first major championship 58-46 before a record crowd of 18,496. (SHU Archives.)

ZENITH. The 1952–1953 Seton Hall men's basketball team won the NIT Championship at a time when it was the premier postseason tournament in the sport. Seton Hall also ended the year with a 31-7 record and was ranked second in the nation by the Associated Press and United Press International polls. The season-ending banquet provided a capstone as Archbishop Thomas Boland of Newark and Msgr. John McNulty, president of Seton Hall, blessed the team. Les Fries, one of Seton Hall's first star players, served as the moderator, and coach Russell and the team were the honorees. Included on this squad were Henry Bockrath, Harry Brooks, Dick Brownley, Henry Cooper, Walter Dukes (co-captain), Gus Eppinger, Bill Hammersley, Mickey Hannon, Bill Loeffler, Ronnie Marra, Jack Milani, Ronnie Nathanic, Joe O'Hare, Richie Regan (co-captain), Arnie Ring, Charles Travers, and Cappy Trowbridge. (Courtesy of SHU Sports Information.)

The Setonian

(Sec. 34.65(e) P. L. & R.)

OFFICIAL UNDERGRADUATE NEWSPAPER OF SETON HALL UNIVERSITY

VOL. XXVII No. 9   MONDAY, MARCH 16, 1953   SOUTH ORANGE, N. J.

Seton Hall 1953 NIT Champions

Cagers Defeat Manhattan; Hall Shines in 74-56 Win

By JIM KISSANE

The Pirates advanced to the NIT finals by ripping Manhattan 74-56 last Thursday night, in the second game of a semi-final-doubleheader. In the first contest St. John's earned the right to play Seton Hall for the NIT championship by toppling highly-favored Duquesne 64-55.

Tom Carroll hit with a jump shot to put Manhattan off to a 2-0 lead against the Pirates. However Walt Dukes knotted the count with a layup. Harry Brooks followed with a side set and a layup and Ron Nathanic found the range with a long set to push Setonia into an 8-2 lead. Manhattan bounced right back. Andy McGowan converting a pair of layups and Junius Kellogg scoring two free throws, to tie the score at 8-all. Brooks retaliated with a layup and push shot to give the Hall a 12-8 advantage. After McGowan brought the Manhattan deficit to two points with a pair of charity tosses, Dukes bucketed three shots to give the Pirates an 18-10 quarter lead. Manhattan was held scoreless for the last six minutes of the opening period.

First Personal

The second canto was one minute old before the Jaspers committed their first foul of the evening. Carroll on Nathanic made good the attempt but Kellogg's layup and Willard Doran's foul shot cut the Setonia margin to 19-13. Dukes repeated layups and superior rebounding enabled Seton Hall to lead at intermission, 35-25.

Lead Cut

Manhattan ripped off seven straight points at the outset of the second half, cutting the count to 35-32. However, Hank Cooper tallied on a pass from Dukes and Hannon tipped in a rebound. Kellogg then dropped in a layup and foul, making it 39-35. After two free throws by Dukes, McGowan flashed in for a follow-up of a missed layup and Doran looped in a long set. But a couple of quick goals by Richie Regan and Arnie Ring widened the gap and the Pirates held a 48-43 lead at the end of the third period.

All Over

In the last quarter Setonia drew away from the Jaspers steadily and began to substitute freely to hold the score down.

Playing before a record throng of 18,496 who turned out, expecting to see a tooth and nail battle between the two finalists, the Pirates won rather handily. The Pirates top-seeded tourney team, became the first top-seeded squad to turn the trick since St. Louis accomplished the feat five years ago. On such a joyous note the long 33-game season ended, Setonia sweeping 31 of their contests, lone setbacks coming at the hands of Dayton and Louisville after the Pirates went undefeated through their first 27 games. Although Dukes got the MVP award, Richie Regan, Arnie Ring, Harry Brooks, and Ronnie Nathanic shared equally in the glory.

The Hall captured the lead after three minutes had elapsed in the opening period and was on its way. After falling behind 6-3 the Pirates caught up and went ahead of St. John's 11-6. Seton never surrendered that lead. They were ahead 14-6 at the end of the first canto and 24-15 at halftime.

Seton Hall turned in as masterful a defensive exhibition as the NIT has ever witnessed in its long 16-year history. The Pirates held the Redmen scoreless until eight minutes had gone by in the second session. Setonia led at intermission, however, not solely as a result of its cloak-like defensive play. St. John's was able to hit on only 17 per cent of its shots in the first half, while Seton Hall found the range with 26 per cent of their attempts from the floor.

The Redmen capitalized on four straight passing lapses by the Pirates in the third quarter to cut to 31-26. Nathanic replaced Mickey Hannon in the Hall lineup and immediately dropped in a one hand push shot and Seton ripped off five more points and that was the ball game. At one point in the last period, the Pirates maintained a 16-point bulge.

Dukes, closing out one of the very best collegiate careers anyone ever had, which saw him named to just about everyone's All-American team, scored 21 points and picked off 20 rebounds. Regan, also ending an amazing collegiate career, notched 13 points and whipped seven scoring passes. His tournament play was simply great. Ring, only a sophomore, performed infinitely well off the boards capturing 22 rebounds, two more than Dukes.

Pirates Down St. Johns in Finale At Madison Square Garden, 58-46

By JIM KISSANE

After a long, tedious struggle over the years to reach the very top in the basketball world, Seton Hall University finally made it. Led by their great All-American Walter Dukes, who was unanimously voted by the Metropolitan sportcaster and scribes the tournament's most valuable player, the Pirates crushed St. John's Cinderella squad by a convincing 58-46 margin Saturday night at Madison Square Garden to capture the 1953 National Invitation Tournament.

Happy Days Are Here Again

After beating Niagara, Manhattan and Saint John's respectively, for the NIT championship, the boys, along with Coach Russell, let loose in the locker room. The victory over St. John's brought the season's record to 31-2.

Correction

The picture with the March of Dimes story, in the March 6th issue, failed to list the names. They were, from left to right, Capt. Ralph Tross, George Schofield, and his mother, Mrs. Schofield.

EXTRA EXTRA! The banner headlines and accompanying text found in this copy of the March 16, 1953 *Setonian* say it all about the 1952–1953 championship squad, including the starring lineup of Dukes, Regan, Hannon, Brooks, Nathanic, and Ring. As a young star on this team, Arnie Ring simply said of the 1952–1953 season, "The press was after you, the fans were great and it was a great experience to go through!" (SHU Archives.)

RICHIE REGAN. Known as the "Cat" and considered one of the finest playmakers in school history, Regan has been affiliated with the Seton Hall basketball program as a player, coach, administrator, and supporter of the Pirates from 1949 to the present. Regan began his hoops career as an All-State performer at West Side High School in Newark during the late 1940s. He enrolled at Seton Hall and became a starter on the varsity team from 1950 to 1953. He served as team co-captain of the 1952–1953 squad and earned a career scoring total of 1,167 points. After graduation, Regan joined the Marine Corps and played ball at Parris Island and Quantico before joining the Rochester Royals (drafted in the first round) from 1955 to 1957. During his two-year NBA stint, Regan averaged 7.8 points per game and earned a spot as captain on the 1956–1957 All-Star team. Regan came back to South Orange during the late 1950s as the freshmen coach before taking over the varsity job from 1960 to 1970. He also earned a master's degree from the school prior to becoming athletic director from 1970 to 1985 and executive director of the Pirate Blue organization thereafter. Richie Regan was elected to the Seton Hall Athletic Hall of Fame in 1973, and his No. 12 jersey has been permanently retired by the university. (Courtesy of SHU Sports Information)

A One Hander. An effort to drive the lane made by Arnie Ring (No. 18) results in a clear shot at the basket in 1953 action. The Pirates of 1953–1954 featured star players Harry Brooks and Mickey Hannon, who also served as co-captains on this team. Brooks tallied 856 points over the course of his Seton Hall career and a 10.7 scoring average per game in 80 contests between 1951 and 1954. Brooks was named to the Seton Hall Athletic Hall of Fame in 1979. (SHU Archives.)

Air Setonia. This is an early Michael Jordon–style move to the basket by Ed Petrie (No. 22) for a quick two against Loyola on February 15, 1954, as the Pirates beat the Ramblers 72-63. Seton Hall has a long history of playing schools outside of New Jersey and the mid-Atlantic region, including fellow Catholic colleges and universities. Even though Seton Hall is the largest diocesan university in the United States, they played many schools affiliated with the Society of Jesus (Jesuits), which produced many of the finest teams in college basketball history, such as Canisius, Fordham, Holy Cross, Marquette, St. Joseph's, San Francisco, and their cross-county rival St. Peter's. The Pirates had a 283-203 record against Jesuit-affiliated schools up through the end of the 2001–2002 season. (SHU Archives.)

FULL EXTENSION. Bill "Stretch" Runge makes the grab for a loose ball against St. Bonaventure in Madison Square Garden on February 4, 1954. Brown Indian star Mal Duffy, who scored 1,029 points in his college career between 1952 and 1955, had the benefit of playing at Seton Hall as a freshman in 1951 before transferring to the Franciscan school in Olean, New York, where he eventually earned an athletic scholarship. Duffy, who had unique perspective as both a Seton Hall player and opponent, said of the mid-1950s Pirates that they fostered "outstanding teams and 'Honey' Russell was a strict coach." (SHU Archives.)

A FLASH CLASH. Ed Petrie (No. 22) does battle with the Red Flash of St. Francis on March 12, 1955, in the first round of the NIT, but Seton Hall lost 89-78. This marked Seton Hall's fifth appearance in the NIT, but St. Francis, led by their star Maurice "the Magnificent" Stokes, made it to the semifinals that year. Stokes was selected by the Rochester Royals in the first round of the 1955 NBA draft and played professional ball until 1958, when he suffered from a tragic illness that left him physically infirm until his death in 1970. A symbol of courage, Stokes still remains an inspiration to basketball fans everywhere. (SHU Archives.)

MICHAEL HANNON. Popularly known as "Mickey," Michael Hannon played at Seton Hall from 1952 to 1954. Hannon was the first winner of the Most Popular Basketball Player Contest, sponsored by the *Setonian* in 1954. He still holds the freshman scoring record with 666 points for the 1949–1950 team, which had a 39-1 season record. In addition to stellar play on the court, Hannon also played right field on the baseball team and hit .355 during his senior year. Injuries plagued him throughout his career. Still, coach Russell said Hannon was a "truly great natural athlete [and] a totally dedicated and intense competitor." Hannon was elected to the Seton Hall Athletic Hall of Fame in 1975. (SHU Archives.)

ARNIE RING. Another star of the early 1950s, the Brooklyn-born Arnie Ring was a forward on Seton Hall teams from 1951 to 1955 and served as co-captain of the 1954–1955 squad. Known primarily for his rebounding ability and recovery of loose balls, Ring also contributed on the offensive side of the court with 682 career points in 87 games. Perhaps his most memorable game came against Niagara in the first round of the 1953 NIT, when he scored 15 points and pulled down 10 boards before posting a 21-rebound performance against St. John's in the final game. Ring noted, "Just to break in was a great experience," and this later translated into election to the Seton Hall Athletic Hall of Fame in 1980. (SHU Archives.)

THE 1953–1954 TEAM. This squad finished the season with a 13-10 year, which was considered a rebuilding season after several members of the senior-laden 1953 team graduated that spring. The Pirates had a number of memorable wins that season and participated in the school's first in-season tournament, the Dixie Classic from December 28 through 30, in which they suffered a first-round loss to the North Carolina State Wolfpack but rebounded to earn a pair of wins against the University of North Carolina 73-63 and Tulane 77-68 in the consolation rounds. Pictured, from left to right, are the following: (front row) Mickey Hannon, and Harry Brooks (co-captain); (back row) Ed Petrie, Henry Bockrath, Arnie Ring, Frank Minaya, Bill Runge, and Ron Nathanic (co-captain). (SHU Archives.)

THE 1954–1955 TEAM. This squad went 17-9 during the year and was the first in a string of three successive teams to earn an NIT invitation. The team defeated such schools as Roanoke 93-62, Wheaton 84-65, Gonzaga 92-70, and Western Kentucky 98-85 before losing to St. Francis in the first round of the NIT. This squad, under the helm of coach Russell, featured Ed Chesney, Joe Damato (equipment manager), Marty Farrell, Dick Gaines, Hugh Gallagher, Charles "Red" Gorman, Johnny Keller, Richie Long (co-captain), Charley Lorenzo, Frank Minaya, Ronnie Nathanic, Ed Petrie, Bill Petrillo, Arnie Ring (co-captain), Bill Runge, and Charles Travers. (SHU Archives.)

DICK GAINES. Mainstay of the mid-1950s Pirates, Dick Gaines played for the varsity team from 1954 to 1957. Gaines scored 1,511 career points at Seton Hall and averaged 20.3 points per game in the 1955–1956 season and 21.1 the following year. He earned various honors, including the MVP trophy for the Richmond Invitational Tournament and was a Look Magazine All-American team member in 1955. He was selected by the Syracuse Nationals in the seventh round of the 1957 NBA draft and played many years in the Eastern League before election to the Seton Hall Athletic Hall of Fame in 1978. (SHU Archives.)

A VERTICAL LEAP. The referee positions himself, and the trailing Musketeer defender gasps in disbelief as Dick Gaines (No. 9) takes off for a basket in the course of a 84-73 Seton Hall victory over Xaiver in this January 10, 1956 game. Gaines had further personal success against the Ohio school a year later when he registered a 30-point performance in the opening round of the 1957 NIT. Counted among the Pirates for 1955–1956 were Ron Berthasavage, Ed Chesney, Tony Comeleo, Marty Farrell, Dick Gaines, Hugh Gallagher, Richie Long, Charley Lorenzo, Julius Nicolai, Ed Petrie (captain), Bill Petrillo, Tom Regan, Don Roberts, Bill Runge, Vince Ryan, Paul Szczech, and Noel Taylor. (SHU Archives.)

A FACE-OFF. A game-opening center tip is contested as the Pirates (in white) do battle with the opposition in 1956, the year Seton Hall University celebrated its centennial anniversary. The atmosphere of the arena was expressed by John Ligos, a player during the late 1940s and a 1984 Seton Hall Athletic Hall of Fame inductee. He noted, "Seton Hall was a great place to play because of the local publicity, there was great crowds, and a strong team and a phenomenal experience." The 1955–1956 campaign was a success, and the Pirates went 20-5 and earned an NIT appearance, where they defeated Marquette in the first round 96-78 before falling to St. Joseph's. (SHU Archives.)

A MOVE UPCOURT. Hugh Gallagher (No. 4) brings the ball upcourt in the season opener of the 1955–1956 campaign against the University of Toronto on December 1, 1955. This game ended in favor of the Pirates 93-60 and is part of the 5-0 mark Seton Hall has against Canadian colleges. Various star players emerged for Seton Hall in this era, including Ed Petrie, who was named to the All-Metropolitan team in 1956 and was drafted by the New York Knicks prior to earning a place in the Seton Hall Athletic Hall of Fame in 1978. Also teaming up with the Pirates during the mid-1950s were Harry "Happy" Brooks (nicknamed by his teammates because of his "poker face"), who was 15th in the nation in scoring in 1953 (and drafted by the Baltimore Bullets in 1954) along with Ron "Nate" Nathanic, who was 10th in the nation that same year. (SHU Archives.)

PROFESSOR RUSSELL. Coach Russell doubled as a member of the Seton Hall faculty as a physical fitness instructor for several years. Here, he is in the midst of a "chalk talk" and draws the position of a man inside the keyhole during this 1955 skull session. An assessment of Russell's instructional technique can be found in a 1936 *Setonian* article, which reads, "Russell is more than an ordinary coach, he is a professor of court strategy and technique. Patient, beyond discretion, he takes pleasure in ironing out the difficulties of the most obscure candidate for the varsity. . . . He has spent hours on fundamentals." Russell's philosophy was "The boys are learning the professional style of play rapidly. Conservation of energy and 'mind over matter' are the keynotes of this peculiar type of court conduct." His final words of wisdom for young players were "If it doesn't look like a ball, don't go out with it!" (SHU Archives.)

ED COPOLA. Esteemed athletic trainer for Seton Hall University basketball teams from 1946 to 1984, Ed Copola also worked at Seton Hall Preparatory during the 1940s. He had a tour of duty as intramural director at the college during the early 1960s, prior to earning an honorary membership in the Seton Hall Athletic Hall of Fame in 1977. (SHU Archives.)

THE 1956–1957 TEAM. This team had another winning season that resulted in a 17-10 ledger but ended in a first-round loss to Xaiver in the NIT. Nattily attired in their team blazers, these players include, from left to right, the following: (front row) Dick Gaines, Richie Buckelew, Lionel Holder, and Ronnie Berthasavage; (middle row) Paul Szczech and Jules Niccolai; (back row) Vinnie Ryan, Charlie Lorenzo, and Phil Samuels. Team members Dick Brightman, Ed Chesney, Tony Comeleo, Tom Cross, Vince Duffy, Dick Farrell, Marty Farrell, and Lionel Holder are absent from this photograph. Charlie Lorenzo was a star player who specialized in the one-handed shot. He had 775 career points and a place in the Seton Hall Athletic Hall of Fame by 1979. (SHU Archives.)

A VANTAGE POINT. This is the view that WSOU broadcaster John Musilli had as he called the Seton Hall-Albright game on January 5, 1957, which resulted in a Pirate victory 92-72. Players, coaches, referees, and the rooting section alike noted that the 12-foot foul lane replaced the 6-foot lane of past years, as seen in this photograph. The 1957–1958 season was a down year of 7-19 but featured some outstanding performances and victories, including ones over Roanoke 68-51, Scranton 61-60, Colby 67-53, and Lafayette 76-75. (SHU Archives.)

OPERATION "BIG O." On January 9, 1958, Seton Hall played the University of Cincinnati at Madison Square Garden and was defeated 118-54. This was one of the worst losses in Seton Hall history but came at the hands of a Bearcat team that featured future hall of famer Oscar Robertson (No. 12), who played with the Cincinnati Royals after graduation. Bearcat coach George Smith was accused of poor sportsmanship for leaving his starting team in the whole game, but one future Seton Hall alumnus that evening admired the play of Robertson. Young Richard Vitale said he was possibly the greatest player ever. Gladys Gooding added background music and played the Seton Hall alma mater on the organ, which was a switch from her usual gig as the organist at Ebbets Field for the Brooklyn Dodgers during the early 1950s. (SHU Archives.)

OBLIQUE AIM. This unique underhanded shot is made by Paul Szczech against the Hilltoppers of Western Kentucky University led by All-American Ralph Crosthwaite (No. 55) at Madison Square Garden on December 19, 1957. Tabbed the "Blonde Bomber" and the "Sunshine Kid," Szczech was a hero to famed announcer Dick Vitale in high school. As he recounted in his autobiography, Vitale used to call WSOU during the postgame show to advise coach Russell to play Szczech more often. Other Pirates who suited up during the 1957–1958 season included Ron Berthsavage, Richie Buckelew, Tom Cross, Vince Duffy, Hugh Dunnion, Connie Egan, Barry Epstein, Seth Hicks, Lionel Holder, Julie Nicolai, Bill Onder, Don Roberts, Jack Rowley, Vinnie Ryan, and Phil Samuels. (SHU Archives.)

THE TEMPLE OF DOOM. A memorable game in Seton Hall basketball history came on January 18, 1957, as the Pirates beat coach Harry Litwack's Temple Owls 66-59 in Walsh Gymnasium. Here, Tom Cross (No. 14) and Marty Farrell (No. 12) do battle with Temple's Jay Norman and All-American Guy Rodgers. Seton Hall would again best Temple in 1959 (68-66) en route to a 13-10 record and record-ending five-game winning streak, beating Long Island University 43-38, Detroit 53-59, Albright 76-52, and Georgetown 89-83 (in overtime). (SHU Archives.)

Four

RECONSTRUCTION
1960–1979

BASKETBALL 101. Originally titled "The Wisdom of Experience," this photograph showcases the bond between the academic and athletic sides of college basketball. Msgr. John J. Dougherty (president of Seton Hall from 1959 to 1969) provides a few words of inspiration and advice prior to the University of Toronto game on December 2, 1959, which signaled the start of the season. That first Pirate team to take the court during the decade went 16-7 and sported victories over such foes as Rider 71-62, Yeshiva 76-50, St. Francis 85-83, Loyola 69-58, Fordham 83-73, Georgetown 80-77, and Niagara 78-74. Seton Hall had an abundance of success between 1939 and 1963, and the Pirates placed ninth on the college basketball most wins list with a 433-178 record (.709 winning percentage), marking the finish of the first successful era in Pirate hoops history. Monsignor Dougherty himself was elected to the Seton Hall Athletic Hall of Fame in 1978. (SHU Archives.)

HONEY'S LAST HURRAH. In the last game of the 1959–1960 season, Seton Hall beat longtime rival St. Peter's College in Jersey City 91-67 to end Honey Russell's coaching career on a high note. Russell earned his 300th coaching victory in 1960, which included stints at Manhattan College during World War II and as the first sideline manager for the Boston Celtics from 1946 to 1949. At Seton Hall, Russell's overall record was 295-129 with a .696 winning percentage during his two tours of duty from 1936 to 1943 (101-32) and 1949 to 1960 (194-97). He was elected to the Naismith Memorial Basketball Hall of Fame in 1964 and the Seton Hall Athletic Hall of Fame by 1973. (SHU Archives.)

CROWD CONTROL. This is an early version of the wave displayed by the Setonia faithful at Walsh Gymnasium in 1960. Those who followed the Pirates during the 1960–1961 season bore witness to various individual victories as Seton Hall posted a 15-9 record. The team participated in its first Holiday Festival Tournament at Madison Square Garden between December 27 and 31, 1960, and lost in the first round to eventual national champions Ohio State 97-57 (a team whose starters John Havilcek, Jerry Lucas, Larry Siegfried, and Bobby Knight were drafted into the NBA) but rebounded to defeat Providence in the second round 92-83 before upsetting the St. Joseph's Hawks 91-83 for the consolation game title. (SHU Archives.)

THE 1959–1960 TEAM. Included on this squad are Joe Bellontine, Frank Besson, Bill Brooks, Ed Coppola (trainer), Hugh Dunnion, Hank Furch, Hank Gunter, Art Hicks, Seth Hicks, Phil Keemer, John Kielbiowski, Don Lane, Ron Olender, Gary Roettger (manager), Walt Rouse, Jack Rowley, John Russell (head coach), Al Senavitis, and Ken Walker. (Angie Marotta is not pictured.) This team was led in points by Art Hicks (393), a transfer from Northwestern University, and Ken Walker, a 5-foot 11-inch guard who earned a place on the Little Men All-America team (for those under 6 feet tall) during the 1958–1959 season. (SHU Archives.)

THE PATERSON PIRATES. Seton Hall was originally located in Madison, New Jersey, from 1856 to 1860 before the permanent move to South Orange. The university again expanded its operations during the mid-20th century to include a number of satellite campuses throughout the state. The Paterson campus (christened the "Silk Mill Setonians") had its own competitive basketball team that began play in 1954 and competed at the Division III level against mostly fellow Garden State schools. This squad was coached for a number of years by Jim Comerford, who played at St. Bonaventure College during the early 1940s and even had eight points in a 1942 game against the Seton Hall Wonder Five. He guided such players as Tony Lagos, Ed Orovitz, and Ed Vreeswyk. (SHU Archives.)

DRIVING THE LANE. Seton Hall's Art Hicks splits through a pair of Roanoke College defenders to put up a finger roll at the basket. Kenny Walker (No. 35) looks on in this December 5, 1959 contest, which the Pirates won 109-67. The early 1960s was a period when Seton Hall was able to crack the century mark in team scoring at various times. Between 1960 and 1962, the Pirates accomplished the feat against Boston College 105-87 (1960), Fairfield 100-96 (1962), St. Peter's 101-78 (1962), St. Francis 100-82, and Scranton 120-100 (January 26, 1962), which still stands as the all-time single game record in program history. (SHU Archives.)

AN UNCONTESTED SHOT. At 5 feet 10 inches tall, Ralph Mezza shows moxy as he cuts through a trio of Fairleigh Dickinson defenders in this 1960 contest won by the Pirates. Prior to the Seton Hall–Rider game in December 1961, a young Bronc player named Richard "Digger" Phelps (who later gained fame as Notre Dame head coach and ESPN analyst) said of the Pirates, "For their size, I think Seton Hall has one of the best teams in the East." (SHU Archives.)

COACH RICHIE REGAN. In March 1960, Richie Regan succeeded Honey Russell as the head coach of the Pirates. Regan was hired by athletic director Fr. Thomas Fahy, who later became university president and earned an honorary selection to the Seton Hall Athletic Hall of Fame in 1975. After serving as the freshman coach from 1958 to 1960, Regan signed a 2-year contact in 1960 that led to a 10-year run. He finished in 1970 with a 112-131 record. As a tribute, the field house located inside Walsh Gymnasium was named in honor of Regan and his late wife, Sheila. Regan's second wife, Sue (Dilley), was the first head coach of the women's basketball team from 1973 to 1985. (SHU Archives.)

CAPTAINS HOOK. "The Good Ship Setonia" was a catchy expression used in various press accounts of the team, and, as with any crew, it always has a captain. Captains were usually chosen by player vote, or appointed by the coach in certain instances. Seton Hall featured game captains from 1903 to 1913 and in various seasons though 1994, when an individual or two could not be chosen. The first full-time captain selected was Peter Jones in 1913, and there have been a number who have served multiple years. Flanking coach Regan in this photograph are Hank Furch (left) and Al Senavitis, who led the 1961–1962 squad. (SHU Archives.)

WHO IS THAT DAPPER DANDY, BABY? Before becoming an expert on college basketball, Richard Vitale (better known as "Dickie V") graduated from Seton Hall University, Paterson Campus, with a management degree in 1962. During his college years, Vitale was active in various campus activities, including the Basketball Booster Club, as sports editor of the *Hall's Echo,* and the Management Club. Vitale (shown here sixth from the left in the back row) played a year of basketball at Roanoke College before transferring to Seton Hall and took his passion for the game through various coaching positions before joining ESPN as a basketball commentator in 1979. Also known for his humanitarian efforts on behalf of the V Foundation for Cancer Research, he noted in his book *Holding Court,* "I wouldn't trade my [Seton Hall] degree for anything." (SHU Archives.)

TIME-OUT TALES. Coach Regan lectures his players during a break in action during this early-1960s game. Between 1960 and 1962, Seton Hall had a number of players who saw service in court wars, including Frank Besson, Bill Brooks, Jim Burkhardt, Randy Chave, Dan Coombs, Hank Furch, Hank Gunter, Art Hicks, Phil Kecemer, Domenik Klein, Philip Meshinsky, Ralph Mezza, Mike Murray, Ron Olender, George Pavlick, Gerry Reidy, Al Senavitis, Golden Sunkett, Ken Walker, Nick Werkman, and Les Wormach. The first annual alumni game was played in December 1961, and the total of former Pirate players has continued to mount ever since. (SHU Archives.)

REBOUND OR SETBACK. The darkest hour in the history of Seton Hall basketball came in 1961, when two members of the team were implicated in a point-shaving scandal that rocked the program. New York district attorney Frank Hogan (who was involved with the 1951 scandal) was involved with this probe involving 37 different players from 22 schools. A meeting of the University Athletic Council resulted in various internal sanctions imposed on the program. This included a plan where no postseason invitations would be accepted for 10 years or in-season tournaments for 5. Only games against schools within the mid-Atlantic or New England region were scheduled, there were fewer scholarships, and limited media coverage was given until the early 1970s. (SHU Archives.)

SMASH-MOUTH BASKETBALL. Seton Hall player Golden "Sunny" Sunkett (No. 22) takes the ball and inadvertently hits a Purple Eagle defender. The Pirates defeated Niagara 81-74 in this February 14, 1963 contest. Seton Hall basketball teams playing during the 1963 calendar year earned placement on various all-time top 10 statistical lists in program history, including eighth in all-time victory margin (+6.7), third in scoring average (79.6), and first in rebound average (60.3). All-time team records in other categories over the years include points scored 1988–1989 (3,107), field goal percentage 1957–1958 (.608), and lowest total points by opponents 1948–1949 (1,321). (SHU Archives.)

THE 1961–1962 TEAM. This squad went 15-9 in a season featuring victories over Southern Illinois 74-73, Portland 93-82, and Detroit 93-88 in what were the last intersectional games played by Seton Hall for a decade. The Pirates also made a national impact by compiling an 88.1 scoring average, which was third in the NCAA and nation that year. Pictured, from left to right, are Mike Murray, Randy Chave, Dom Klein, Al Senavitis, Nick Werkman, George Pavlick, Richie Regan (head coach), John Murphy (assistant coach), Joe Bellantine, Jim Burkhardt, Hank Furch, Phil Meshinsky, Dan Coombs, and Gerry Reidy. (SHU Archives.)

RIVALRY REDUX. A textbook jump shot is made by Nick Werkman (No. 44) against the Providence Friars on February 15, 1964, as Al Senavitis (No. 32) looks on. The Friar player (No. 51) attempting to make the block is longtime Seton Hall nemesis John Thompson, who went on to coach the Georgetown Hoyas from 1972 to 1999. Throughout the latter part of the 20th century, a number of individuals affiliated with the Big East either as a player or coach (and sometimes both) had an impact on Pirate basketball, including, ironically enough, former Syracuse star Louis Orr, who was named Seton Hall head coach in 2001. (SHU Archives.)

AL SENAVITIS. Al Senavitis, a native of Bethlehem, Pennsylvania, was a member of the team from 1959 to 1962 and left South Orange after four years with 904 career points and a place in the Seton Hall Athletic Hall of Fame in 1982. Known for his unorthodox one-handed jump shot, Senavitis averaged 17 points per game in 1961–1962 as part of a young squad, many of whom returned the following year. The 1962–1963 roster included Joseph Barlik, Randy Chave, Tony Cuccolo, Richie Dec, Domenik Klein, Mike McMahon, Philip Meshinsky, Mike Murry, Robert Plocinik, Gerry Reidy, Harry Slaton, Golden Sunkett, Nick Werkman, and Les Wormach. (SHU Archives.)

SCORING STYLE. Seton Hall player Harry Slaton (No. 24) goes up for bank shot off the backboard in this 1963 game at Walsh Gymnasium as Gerry Reidy (No. 14) and Nick Werkman (No. 44) look on. The 1962–1963 season was one in which the Pirates went 16-7 and earned victories over St. Anslem's 90-70, Loyola 75-57, Boston University 69-64, Rider 79-42, Boston College 61-53, Catholic University of America 80-75, Upsala 94-71, St. Francis 101-85, and Georgetown 78-76. (SHU Archives.)

"THE QUICK." Affectionately known as "Tricky Nick" and "the Twist," the second most prolific scorer in Seton Hall basketball history with 2,273 career points was Nick Werkman. A product of Trenton Catholic High School, Werkman won All-State honors and led the Golden Wave to the New Jersey Parochial Catholic title in 1960 before enrolling at Seton Hall. Werkman played on the Pirate varsity from 1962 to 1964 and served as co-captain during the 1963–1964 season. In between practice and games, Werkman was a premed major who also participated in various extracurricular activities, including the Art Club, National Student Association, and Setonian Film Society prior to graduation in 1964. He led the Pirates in scoring for three straight years with a 32-point-per-game average. Werkman also rated nationally on a yearly basis, ranking third in 1962, second in 1964, and first in 1963 with individual season averages of 32, 33.2, and 29.5, respectively. Werkman is the first (and only one of three) Seton Hall players ever to eclipse the 2,000-plus mark in career points in a three-year career, even before the three-point shot came into play. (Courtesy of SHU Sports Information.)

AWARD WINNER. Msgr. Edward Fleming, executive vice president and former chairman of the University Athletic Council, presents Nick Werkman with an award *c*. 1964 as coach Regan looks on approvingly. Monsignor Fleming entered the Seton Hall Athletic Hall of Fame 13 years after Nick Werkman achieved the honor in 1973, but this was not the end of the honors for "the Quick" and other Seton Hall players. Werkman won the Haggerty Award for top player in the Metropolitan area in 1964, was a Second Team All-American in 1963, and Third Team selection by the Associated Press and United Press International a year later. His No. 44 jersey has been permanently retired by Seton Hall. (SHU Archives.)

TOUR DE FORCE. Gliding to the hoop, Nick Werkman (No. 44) puts up the ball over a crouching defender in early 1960s action. By graduation, Werkman held 25 individual Seton Hall basketball records, including the most free throws made in a career (649 out of 980) and the number of points (52) and field goals (21) made in a single game (against the University of Scranton on January 29, 1964). After graduating from Seton Hall, Werkman was drafted by the defending world champion Boston Celtics in 1965 but ended up playing for eight years in the Eastern League prior to coaching basketball at Stockton State College in Pomona, New Jersey, during the 1970s. (SHU Archives.)

OVER THE BACK. Seton Hall player Nick Werkman (No. 44) blocks out a St. Bonaventure defender in this early-1960s contest. Al Senavitis (No. 32) looks on at the right side during this next-to-last game played by the Pirates at Madison Square Garden until 1969. The 1963–1964 campaign concluded with a 13-12 record, the last winning season for Seton Hall before the 1973–1974 season. (SHU Archives.)

THE 1963–1964 TEAM. Pirates of the 1963–1964 season pictured here are, from left to right, Bob Plocinik, Randy Chave, Golden Sunkett (co-captain), Richie Regan (head coach), Nick Werkman (co-captain), Gerry Reidy, Joe Barlik, and Harry Slaton. Team members Anthony Cuccolo, Richie Dec, John Dunleavy, John Evers, Jim Kenney, and Charley Mitchel are not pictured. The stars on this team included Randy Chave, who served as co-captain in 1962–1963, and Golden Sunkett, who still holds the single season assist record with 197 (an average of 8.57) in 1962–1963. In addition, Anthony Cuccolo, who scored 921 career points, joined the Seton Hall Athletic Hall of Fame in 1991. (SHU Archives.)

RICHIE DEC. Richie Dec was a hometown player who lived in the South Orange area and went to school at Seton Hall as a premed and chemistry major. Dec, who earned All-State and All-American accolades at Seton Hall Preparatory, enrolled at the university in the early 1960s and went on to play for the Pirates from 1962 to 1965. In this span, he never missed a game and played in 73 overall during his days on the Seton Hall varsity. He also led the Pirates in scoring during the 1964–1965 season with a 16.9 average and earned 1,123 career points prior to earning a place in the Seton Hall Athletic Hall of Fame in 1979. (Courtesy of SHU Sports Information.)

CHARLES MITCHEL. Here, Charles Mitchel (No. 32) looks downcourt, pondering his options while maintaining possession in this March 3, 1965 game against Villanova. Mitchel (known as "Mitch" or the "Columbus Comet") was described as "an excellent shot and an adroit passer" in his career at Seton Hall from 1963 to 1966, which resulted in a 944 career point total. Dr. Mitchel is now the chairman of administration and supervision in the College of Education and Human Services at Seton Hall and was a Seton Hall Athletic Hall of Fame inductee in 1991. (SHU Archives.)

JET PROPELLED. This mid-1960s photograph shows the Pirates taking to the air for a short flight en route to a road game. Seton Hall has won a number of road games, over a dozen in which they scored more than 100 points, including a record of 109 against John Carroll in 1953. Those who played for the Pirates during the 1964–1965 season include Joe Barlik, Tony Cuccolo, Richie Dec (co-captain), John Dunleavy, John Evers, Jim Kenney, Charley Mitchel, Terry Morawski, Denny Parvin, Bob Plocinik, Mark Seymour, Harry Slaton (co-captain), Richie Westover, and Vince Wright. Morawski went on to set the single-season free throw percentage record with .888 (136 of 153) during the 1965–1966 campaign. (SHU Archives.)

REACHING OUT. With outstretched arm and palm, Chris Zier (No. 23) grasps for a loose ball as Larry "Rover" Rovelstad (No. 30) races to assist in this mid-1960s game against St. Peter's College. During the 1964–1965 season, the Pirates clawed their way to a 12-13 record from December through March and defeated Loyola 90-77 in the opener, followed by wins against Fordham 69-67, Long Island University 74-64, Colgate 85-80, Niagara 85-77, St. Peter's 79-78, and a season-ending victory over Iona 71-59. (SHU Archives.)

JOHN SUMINSKI. A star player on the Seton Hall squads of the late 1960s, John Suminski competed for the Pirates from 1966 to 1969. Suminski, a history major, also served as president of his freshman and sophomore classes in between scoring 846 points on the court and attaining lasting recognition as a member of the Seton Hall Athletic Hall of Fame in 1982. Suminski made several layups in his career as part of Pirate point tallies made without benefit of the slam dunk, which was declared illegal in 1967 and restored in match play 10 years later. (SHU Archives.)

BILL SOMERSET. A history and political science major at Seton Hall, Bill Somerset takes a free throw in a game during his tenure as co-captain of the 1967–1968 squad. Somerset and his teammates were on campus at Seton Hall when coeducation was introduced during the fall of 1968. Those who were featured on the player roster between 1965 and 1968 included Brian Blake, Joe Cooke, Tony Cuccolo, Richie Dooley, Jack Dunleavy, John Evers, Kevin Foley, Dan Gregory, Bill Karatz, Gerry Mackey, Charley Mitchel, Terry Morawski, Ken Moss, Bob Mulhern, Larry Rovelstad, Steve Schoenhaus, Mark Seymour, Bill Somerset, Bob Sparks, John Suminski, Mike Wall, Richie Westover, Vince Wright, and Bill Young. (SHU Archives.)

A BLOCK PARTY. Pirate star Ken House (No. 42) tries to block a shot against All-American Bob Lanier of the Final Four–bound St. Bonaventure Bonnies on February 11, 1970. Lanier was just one in a line of outstanding opposing players in the pre–Big East years. The list also included Paul Arizin of Villanova (1950), Bob Cousy of Holy Cross (1947), Dave DeBusschere of Detroit (1961–1962), Ernie DiGregorio of Providence (1971–1973), Tom Gola of LaSalle (1952), John Havilcek of Ohio State (1960), Cedric Maxwell of the University of North Carolina, Charlotte (1977), Jim Paxson of Dayton (1953), Howard Porter of Villanova (1970), Oscar Robertson of Cincinnati (1958), Guy Rodgers of Temple (1958), Phil Sellers of Rutgers (1976), Maurice Stokes of St. Francis in Pennsylvania (1955), and many others. (SHU Archives.)

GERRY MACKEY. Seton Hall player Gerry Mackey goes up for a shot against the U.S. Military Academy during the late 1960s. Mackey was an all-around player during his tenure with the Pirates. He played varsity ball from 1965 to 1968 and sported a 10.6-per-game scoring average and 673 total points during his 63 games in a Seton Hall uniform. (SHU Archives.)

MEL KNIGHT. Nicknamed the "Marvel" due to his superlative ball handling, Mel Knight was one of the finest secondary school players in New Jersey while a player for Seton Hall Preparatory, where he was a scholastic All-State and All-American selection as a senior in 1967. After enrolling at Seton Hall University in 1967, Knight led the freshmen team to a 15-5 record with a 24.7 point average and joined the varsity from 1968 through 1971, but he only appeared in 50 games due to injuries. He scored 775 career points and was described by Dick Vitale as a "Thomas Edison Special" (one who is a creative and innovative player). Knight also attained All-Metropolitan and All-East honors prior to his election to the Seton Hall Athletic Hall of Fame in 1978. He served as the assistant director of athletics at Seton Hall from 1972 to 1975. (SHU Archives.)

ELEVATING PLAY. A drive to the hoop by John Suminski (No. 40) against St. Peter's College on February 15, 1969, results in a deuce, and Peacock player Bob Leckie (No. 11) hits the deck. Although overall seasonal marks recorded during the mid-1960s were mediocre at best, the Pirates never failed to win at least six games per season between 1965 and 1968. Counted among these was a win over Wake Forest 71-70 in the first round of the 1967 Vanderbilt Classic in Nashville, which was Seton Hall's second in-season tournament appearance since 1966. (SHU Archives.)

THE 1968–1969 TEAM. This squad went 9-16 and featured, from left to right, the following: (front row) John Suminski, Kevin Foley, Richie Regan (head coach), Larry Rovelstad, Ken Moss, and Barnett Barmen (manager); (middle row) Joe Cooke, Bob Mulhern, Bill Young, Mike Wall, John Thurston, and Steve Boryczewski; (back row) Bill McCrea, Mel Knight, Marty Murphy, and Gary Cavallo. These individuals teamed up with Frank Cortes, Junior Foy, Ken House, Roger Kindel, Bill McCrea, Bob Mulhern, Ron Wood, and Chris Zier, who are not pictured, and defined the Seton Hall program between 1968 and 1970. (SHU Archives.)

THE 1970–1971 TEAM. This is a midcourt view of the team, which went 11-15. From left to right, they are as follows: (front row) Steve Lavino, Roger Kindel, Frank Cortes, Mel Knight (co-captain), and Paul Caffrey; (back row) Tom Pugliese (assistant coach), Gary Cavallo (co-captain), Bill McCrea, Ken House, Junior Foy, Jim LaCorte, Tom O'Donnell, and Bill Raftery (head coach). This year represented a sort of six degrees of separation for Seton Hall, as the Pirates played Boston College, which was coached by Chuck Daly, who coached Isaiah Thomas with the Detroit Pistons after Thomas was a player for Bobby Knight after Knight coached Army in a loss against Seton Hall, and the Black Knights also lost to Fordham led by player P.J. Carlesimo, who ended up coaching Seton Hall and defeated Knight, Army, and Boston College during his time with the Pirates. (SHU Archives.)

BILL RAFTERY. Named as the head coach in February 1970, Raftery is pictured with Fr. John J. Horgan, former athletic director from 1960 to 1972 and Seton Hall Athletic Hall of Fame inductee in 1976. A popular figure on the South Orange campus, Raftery smiled a lot, attended many functions, and had a strong affinity for the student body during his days at Seton Hall, which lasted until 1981 and resulted in a 154-141 record overall. Prior to assuming the Pirates post, Raftery played basketball at St. Cecilia's High School in Kearny and registered 2,192 points over four years (a state record at the time) and at LaSalle College, where he led the Explorers to an NIT appearance during the 1960s. Raftery also had a tryout with the New York Knicks before moving on to coaching, where he led Fairleigh Dickinson, Madison, for five years before coming to Seton Hall. After retiring as a coach, Raftery became a broadcaster with CBS and ESPN and color commentator for the 2001–2002 Eastern Division Champion New Jersey Nets after his 1984 induction as a member of the Seton Hall Athletic Hall of Fame. (SHU Archives.)

WHAT GOES UP. Seton Hall player Ken House (No. 42) swats for the ball during an early-1970s game. Among the players who shared room on the floor with House from 1971 to 1973 were Mike Buescher, Paul Caffrey, Raymond Clark, Frank Cortes, Tom Flaherty, Junior Foy, Frank Foye, Ollie Hawkins, Roger Kindel, Jim LaCorte, Pete LaCorte, Paul Lape, Steve Lavino, William McFarland, Jim McManus, Tom O'Donnell, John Ramsay, Chris Rzonca, Dick Stukenbroeker, Bill Terry, Ron Wood, and Frank Zelesnik. Included on this squad was Gary Cavallo, who scored 820 points during his career and was elected to the Seton Hall Athletic Hall of Fame in 1978. (SHU Archives.)

KEN HOUSE. Coach Raftery called House his "bread and butter player" who excelled not only on the court but also in the classroom as a history major and dean's list student. He was one of only four Seton Hall players (Dukes, Mosley, and Werkman were the others) to amass over 1,000 points and rebounds in a career, registering 1,670 points and 1,149 rebounds between 1969 and 1972. House also made his mark on the NCAA record books when he ranked 10th in the nation in rebounds with a 15.8 average during the 1969–1970 season. He served as team captain between 1971 and 1972 and took this symbolic picture at the Seton Hall Alumni Bell with coach Raftery. House made the Metropolitan Sports Writers All-Star team in 1971 and 1972 prior to making the Seton Hall Athletic Hall of Fame in 1978. (S.R. Smith and SHU Sports Information.)

THE 1973–1974 TEAM. This congregation went 16-11 on the year and earned its first NIT bid since 1957. Seton Hall resumed a national schedule and achieved success before losing to Memphis State 73-72 in the first round of the NIT. Freshmen were declared eligible to play in varsity games during this season. The Pirates that year, pictured from left to right, included the following: (front row) Pete LaCorte, Tom Flaherty, Paul Lape, Ollie Hawkins, and Frank Foye; (back row) Bill Raftery (head coach), Ed Wozniak (manager), Don Stukenbroeker, Chris Rzonca, Bruce Gardner, Mike Buescher, John Ramsey, Ray Clark, Ed Pohren (assistant manager), Hoddy Mahon (assistant coach), and Boscoe Bell. Bill Terry and Frank Zazzaro are not pictured. (SHU Archives.)

JOHN RAMSEY. Known as "Ram" during his playing days, John Ramsey amassed 1,236 career points for the Pirates between 1972 and 1975. He was part of the Seton Hall basketball renaissance during the 1970s and a third-round draft choice of the New York Knicks in 1975. Other stars for the Pirates from 1974 through 1976 included Mike Buescher, Mike Clay, Marc Coleman, Randy Duffin, Tom Flaherty, Nick Galis, Billy Gardner, Robbie Hall, Ollie Hawkins, Pete Jeremich, Pete LaCorte, Paul Lape, Mike McDonnell, Glenn Mosley, Don Stukenbroeker, Cliff Tracey, Greg Tynes, and Frank Zazzaro. The 1974–1975 Pirates went 16-11 for the season, bowing to St. John's in the first round of their first Eastern Collegiate Athletic Conference (ECAC) Tournament appearance. (Courtesy of SHU Sports Information.)

GLENN MOSLEY. Mosley (No. 34) elevates over Georgetown defenders on January 24, 1976, which contributed to a 102-91 Pirate victory. The six-foot eight-inch center-forward from Newark was nicknamed "Smiles" for his sunny disposition and positive play. Coach Raftery said Mosley was "one of the finest young gentlemen I have ever coached or met." Mosley played for Seton Hall between 1973 and 1977 and, in that time, scored 1,441 points and snared 1,263 rebounds, including his leading mark of 16.3 in the nation during 1976–1977. His 15.2 career average also ranks high on the NCAA all-time list and helped lead talent scouts to South Orange. This resulted in a first-round selection (20th overall) by the Philadelphia 76ers in 1977. Mosley also played on the San Antonio Spurs during the late 1970s and entered the Seton Hall Athletic Hall of Fame in 1984. His No. 34 jersey has been retired by Seton Hall. (*Galleon* yearbook.)

THE 1976–1977 TEAM. The Pirates ended the 1975–1976 season with an 18-9 record. They followed this performance in the 1976–1977 season with an 18-11 mark, a Niagara Tournament Championship, and first-round victory over Army (77-71) in the ECAC Tournament before losing by one point to the University of Massachusetts, Amherst, in the NIT first round that March. The members of the 1976–1977 team are, from left to right, as follows: (front row) Greg Tynes, Nick Galis, Cliff Tracey, Ed Janeczak, and Mike McDonnell; (back row) Bill Raftery (head coach), Jay Boyle, Randy Duffin, Frank Zazzaro, Glenn Mosley, Pete Jeremich, Marc Coleman, John Semerad, and Hoddy Mahon (assistant coach). (SHU Archives.)

THE WINNING TAP. The Pirates see action in this mid-1970s contest as Glenn Mosley controls the ball and teammates wait in anticipation to see how the ball will fall. During the 1977–1978 campaign, Seton Hall was able to register a 16-11 record, including an opening-round win in the Big Sun Tournament against West Virginia 76-73, and earned an ECAC Tournament first-round appearance. (Courtesy of SHU Sports Information.)

RUBBER BAND MAN. A road game in Philadelphia for Seton Hall against Villanova on January 20, 1976, features Robbie Hall (No. 43) grabbing a rebound as Randy Duffin (No. 31) supports his teammate. The Pirates featured a roster of players in 1977–1978 who helped Seton Hall to a 16-11 record. Included on this squad were Andy Arrington, Jay Boyle, Richard Browne, Marc Coleman, John Davis, Randy Duffin, Nick Galis, Pete Jeremich, Scott Langle, Tony Massaro, Dan Mobbs, Dawan Scot, John Semerad, and Greg Tynes. (*Galleon* yearbook.)

GREG TYNES. A six-foot one-inch guard from nearby Orange High School, Tynes entered Seton Hall and played for the Pirates from 1974 to 1978. Tynes scored 2,059 points during the course of his career. He was co-captain of the 1977–1978 team, a season in which he scored 556 points for a 20.5 average while battling a foot injury. Phil Ford, a University of North Carolina All-American who played opposite him in 1975, praised Tynes and said, "He's got style all his own. Inside, outside, anywhere he's a tough man to handle because he's so quick." Tynes was selected by the Boston Celtics in the fifth round of the 1978 draft and was elected to the Seton Hall Athletic Hall of Fame in 1986. (*Galleon* yearbook.)

AN MVP PRESENTATION. The 1977–1978 postseason basketball awards for top players went to Greg Tynes and Robin Cunningham of the women's team. Pictured, from left to right, are an unidentified man, Richie Regan, Greg Tynes, Robin Cunningham, and Dr. Robert T. Conley, former president of Seton Hall. Cunningham, who was the first woman to receive an athletic scholarship to Seton Hall, was a multisport athlete who played softball, tennis, and basketball from 1975 to 1978. She was elected to the Seton Hall Athletic Hall of Fame in 1984, and her No. 32 has been permanently retired. Cunningham has also served as the director of academic support services for student-athletes at Seton Hall since 1984. (SHU Archives.)

NICK GALIS. A star player for the Pirates from 1975 to 1979, Galis notched a 27.5 scoring average in 1979, ranking him third in the nation during his senior year. Galis scored 1,651 points in his career, ranking him ninth on the all-time Seton Hall list. Galis won the New Jersey Senior Award, Haggerty Trophy, and the ECAC Division I Best Player Prize for 1979 prior to his entry into the 1979 NBA draft. He was selected by the Boston Celtics in the fourth round. Galis was elected to the Seton Hall Athletic Hall of Fame in 1991. (Courtesy of SHU Sports Information.)

IN TRAFFIC. This one-handed acrobatic shot by Seton Hall's Nick Galis occurred over a St. John's defender on March 5, 1977, at Madison Square Garden in the second round of the ECAC Tournament. The 1978–1979 campaign that followed resulted in a 16-11 record. The roster included Andy Arrington, Jay Boyle, Richard Browne, Dan Callandrillo, Marc Coleman, John Davis, Nick Galis, Scott Langel, Sam Loftin, Ed Mackiewicz, Tony Massaro, Howard McNeil, Dan Mobbs, John Semerad, and Clark Young. (*Galleon* yearbook.)

THE ENVELOPE, PLEASE. Former Seton Hall head coach Bill Raftery addresses attendees at the Pirate Blue Basketball Awards Banquet in 1995, where he received the John Honey Russell Award as a Pirate basketball alumnus who "truly represents the values of Seton Hall University" in recognition of his accomplishments during the 1970s. Along with the John Honey Russell Award, the William J. Eyres Award goes to an individual who supports the team, and the O. Lawrence Keefe Award is bestowed upon members of the media who cover the Pirates. (Courtesy of SHU Sports Information.)

BLOWING THE WHISTLE. Raftery crouches on the sidelines in coaching mode during a 1970s contest. A number of legendary field generals in the pre–Big East period have also gone to battle with Seton Hall over the years and have contributed to the court strategy and intrigue that make up a basketball game. Such coaches as Clair Bee (Long Island University), Howard Hobson (Yale), Nat Holman (CCNY), Alvin "Doggie" Julian (Holy Cross), Frank Keaney (Rhode Island State), Joe Lapchick (St. John's), Ray Meyer (DePaul), Jim Phelan (Mount St. Mary's), Jack Ramsey (St. Joseph's), Alex Severance (Villanova), and Jim Valvano (Iona) are just a few who have opposed Seton Hall over the years. (*Galleon* yearbook.)

SETON HALL UNIVERSITY
Founded 1856
BASKETBALL PROGRAM

The Pirates
vs.
Boston College
December 11, 1979
WALSH AUDITORIUM

The First
Game Of

THE **BIG EAST**
CONFERENCE

$1.00

INAUGURAL CONTEST. The Big East Conference was born on May 31, 1979, and Seton Hall became a charter member of the league with other schools situated in the northeast United States, including Boston College, Georgetown, Providence, St. John's, Syracuse, and the University of Connecticut. They were joined by Villanova and the University of Pittsburgh during the early 1980s, and this group eventually swelled to include the University of Notre Dame, Rutgers, West Virginia, the University of Miami, and Virginia Tech by the 2001–2002 season. Athletic director Richie Regan brought Seton Hall into the Big East by helping to raise the entrance fee through assistance by generous supporters and university administrators. This game program, featuring artwork by New Jersey artist Bill Canfield, shares space with a banner that proclaims the very first basketball game in league history, but Seton Hall lost to Boston College 82-61. It was not until the following year that the Pirates won their first Big East game against Providence on January 26, 1980, by a score of 64-51. Canfield designed the cover for several Seton Hall basketball media guides during the 1970s and 1980s. (Courtesy of SHU Sports Information.)

Five

RENEWAL
1979–1989

THE 1979–1980 TEAM. The first Seton Hall squad to represent the school in Big East competition poses for a team picture after a practice session. Those who played for coach Raftery on the trailblazing 1979–1980 team included Andy Arrington, Ray Brooks, Richard Browne, Dan Callandrillo, Daryl Devero, Dan Dunne, Steve Grieco, Edward Mackiewicz, Tony Massaro, Howard McNeil, Ray Ortiz, Matt Piccinich, John Tansil, and Clark Young. Counted among the earliest Pirates to attain Big East season-ending accolades was Dan Callandrillo, who was a Second Team All–Big East selection in 1979–1980. The following year, three Pirate players won conference honors and started hosting games at the Brendan Byrne Arena (or Meadowlands Arena, now known as the Continental Airlines Arena), named in honor of the former New Jersey governor and Seton Hall alumnus. The feeling of joining a major conference was summarized by coach Raftery, who stated in 1980, "Without even a full year, the Big East has captured the basketball fan's imagination." (Courtesy of SHU Sports Information.)

CATCH-22. Marc Coleman, a six-foot five-inch forward from East Orange, New Jersey, played for the Pirates from 1975 to 1979. Coleman scored 814 points in his career. He is shown here blocking the shot of former NBA star and current Iona head coach Jeff Ruland when the Pirates played the Gaels on March 1, 1979. Team co-captain (1978–1979) Coleman was described as having a mile-high jumper, which led to his seventh-round selection by the New York Knicks in the 1979 draft. Notice that Coleman sported Seton Hall's famed patriotic uniform of the late 1970s and early 1980s, which featured a red, white, and blue stars and stripes motif. (*Galleon* yearbook.)

HOWARD MCNEIL. Nicknamed "Smooth" for his steady and superlative court play, Howard McNeil, a six-foot nine-inch forward from Philadelphia, played at Seton Hall from 1978 to 1982 and scored 1,057 points as a Pirate. McNeil was a fifth-round draft pick of the Los Angeles Lakers in 1982. Along with McNeil, the 1980–1981 team included Andy Arrington, Tom Brown, Dan Callandrillo, Sir John Collins, Daryl Devero, Dan Dunne, Steve Grieco, Ed Mackiewicz, Tony Massaro, Ray Ortiz, and Matt Piccinich. Many of these players also contributed to the 14-13 1979–1980 season. (Courtesy of SHU Sports Information.)

THE OPENING TOSS! Fans throw streamers onto the unique dark brown floor of Walsh Gymnasium (dubbed the "Snake Pit" during the early 1980s) after the Pirates score their first basket in this 1982 contest. The lost tradition of celebrating a home team's initial field goal with a streamer toss arose to an art form in the Philadelphia Palestra and other campus courts across the nation, but it is now subject to a technical foul. (*Galleon* yearbook.)

FLAG WAVERS. Other forms of basketball-generated celebration, including cheerleading routines and mascots such as the longstanding Pirate (and even a chicken man, which shared duties during the early 1980s), were evident on the sidelines and hit the court during time-outs and halftime shows. The Pirate has also become a fixture at the Meadowlands and on television commercials. Various sources claimed that Seton Hall had the largest banner of its kind in the country by the early 1990s. (S.R. Smith and SHU Sports Information.)

DAN CALLANDRILLO. Known as "Mr. Clutch" for his solid play, Dan Callandrillo was an All-State performer at North Bergen High School and made the successful transition to Seton Hall, where he became a star for the Pirates from 1978 to 1982. Callandrillo was an all-around performer who had a smooth jump shot and strong defensive skills. The six-foot two-inch guard was a consummate team player who noted during his playing days, "I would much rather win than score a lot of points." He is the all-time Seton Hall career steals leader with 260 and ended with 1,985 points overall. Callandrillo had the fourth-highest scoring average in the nation in 1982, and that year he earned First Team All-Metropolitan honors, was named Big East Player of the Year, and earned Third Team All-American recognition. After graduation, Callandrillo was picked in the eighth round of the NBA draft by the Houston Rockets and was enshrined in the Seton Hall Athletic Hall of Fame in 1989. (Courtesy of SHU Sports Information.)

EYEING OPTIONS. Coach Raftery offers encouragement (in the background) as Dan Callandrillo ponders how to proceed past a Syracuse defender in this February 21, 1981 game, in which the Pirates defeated the Orangemen 66-65. The players who went on to represent the Pirates for the 1981–1982 season included Kevin Boyle, Ray Brooks, Tom Brown, Dan Callandrillo, Sir John Collins, Daryl Devero, Dan Dunne, Steve Grieco, Ed Mackiewicz, Tony Massaro, Howard McNeil, Ray Ortiz, and Matt Piccinich. (*Galleon* yearbook.)

AN EXECUTIVE ORDER. Members of the "Baby Brigade," from left to right, include Daryl Devero, Tom Brown, Dr. Edward D'Alessio (university president), Clark Young, and Dan Callandrillo as they pose with the ceremonial first ball. Since Seton Hall first fielded a basketball team in 1903, the university has had 16 different presidents who have kept the program running. (S.R. Smith and SHU Sports Information.)

REBOUND BOUND. This box-out by Pirate Mike Ingram (No. 25) of a Fighting Irish forward is successful as Seton Hall defeated Notre Dame 71-58 in their first-ever meeting on February 18, 1982. Seton Hall went 11-16 during the 1981–1982 season and earned wins over Utah State 85-77 (Kentucky Invitational Tournament), Florida Southern 79-77, and Princeton 75-74. The biggest victory of this period came in Seton Hall's first-ever appearance (and one of the earliest college basketball games held) at the Meadowlands Arena when they defeated the nationally ranked University of Houston 87-85 in an overtime thriller. (*Galleon* yearbook.)

HORACE MAHON. Mahon was a popular coach who was commonly known as "Hoddy" around campus. Prior to his appearance at Seton Hall, Mahon, a graduate of St. Peter's College, led basketball teams at Orange High School, Essex Catholic, and Fordham University. Mahon served as Bill Raftery's assistant coach during the 1970s before taking over the program during the 1981–1982 campaign. After winning his first six games in a row (the best seasonal start for the Pirates since 1961), placards proclaiming "Sign Hoddy Now" were seen throughout Walsh Gymnasium by December. (*Galleon* yearbook.)

A FAMILY AFFAIR. On April 5, 1982, Seton Hall signed a young coach from Scranton, Pennsylvania, named Peter J. Carlesimo (better known as "P.J.") to head its basketball team. Carlesimo played for Fordham University and was a star on the 1970–1971 squad, which went 26-3 and earned an NCAA bid under Richard "Digger" Phelps. Upon graduation in 1971, Carlesimo served as an assistant coach for the Rams from 1971 to 1975, where he learned the craft and molded young players, including budding star of the court and screen Denzel Washington. Carlesimo's first head coaching job came at New Hampshire College from 1975 to 1976 before moving on to Wagner College, where he led the Seahawks between 1976 and 1982. Pictured, from left to right, are Carlesimo, Richie Regan (athletic director), Dr. Edward D'Alessio (university president), and Peter Carlesimo (P.J.'s father and former president of the Metropolitan Intercollegiate Basketball Association). Upon hire, Carlesimo said in an interview, "I am tremendously excited about the opportunity at Seton Hall. The Big East represents the best in college basketball, and I look forward to the challenge." (Courtesy of SHU Sports Information.)

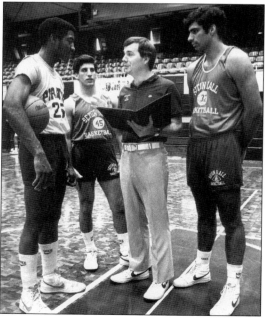

INSTRUCTION BY P.J. "Enthusiastic, knowledgeable, personable, witty" were the adjectives used to describe Carlesimo in the 1984–1985 Seton Hall basketball media guide. This early-1980s look at a Pirate practice shows Carlesimo (center) talking to Mike Ingram (No. 25), Steve Grieco (No. 45), and Dan Dunne (No. 32) at Walsh Gymnasium. In Carlesimo's first year, he guided Seton Hall to a 6-21 season. Players on this team included Kevin Boyle, Roy Brooks, Tom Brown, Ricky Burton, Dan Dunne, Steve Grieco, Mike Ingram, Andre McCloud, Marvin Morris, Ken Powell, Nate Rogers, John Sealy, and Clark Young. This inauspicious start translated into a Big East Coach of the Year award in both 1988 and 1989 and National Coach of the Year recognition in 1989. (*Galleon* yearbook.)

COUNTER COACHING. A sideline view from an early-1980s game shows Carlesimo opposing Boston College and their head coach Gary Williams. During Carlesimo's second season, he amassed a 9-19 record. This team was led by Brad Broussard, Tom Brown, Spencer Bryant, Ricky Burton, Sir John Collins, Ransom Eaves, Mike Jones, Andre McCloud, Marvin Morris, Ken Powell, Nate Rogers, Dan Stefankiewicz, Bob Vogt, Phil Whitaker, and Jim Wood. Carlesimo stayed at Seton Hall and recorded an overall 212-166 mark from 1982 to 1994. He then joined the NBA and coached the Portland Trailblazers and Golden State Warriors during the 1990s before entering the NBC broadcast booth in December 2000. (*Galleon* yearbook.)

BILL BRADLEY. Sen. Bill Bradley was an All-American player at Princeton University from 1961 to 1965. Seton Hall has a longstanding rivalry with Princeton, and the Pirates have an all-time 8-3 record against the Tigers up through the 2001–2002 season. When he was a player with the New York Knicks, Bradley gave a lecture on campus that was publicized by the *Setonian* as an address by a "former Rhodes Scholar [and] future politician" on November 27, 1973. When this prophecy came true five years later, Bradley visited Seton Hall on numerous occasions to discuss political issues and athletic competition, including this 1984 meeting with Msgr. John Petillo (former Seton Hall president) and Fr. James Mannion (seated on left), who served as team chaplain for a number of years. (Courtesy of SHU Sports Information.)

THE 1984–1985 TEAM. This group of Pirates went 10-18 on the year, including wins over Pace 70-51, Central Connecticut 99-78, Hartford 89-63, and two in-season tournament championships (Shawmut Worcester County Classic and San Juan Classic) during December 1984. Pictured are, from left to right, the following: (front row) Brad Broussard, Nate Rogers, Spencer Bryant, Mike Jones, Ransom Eaves, Jim Wood, and James Major; (back row) Ricky Burton, Andre McCloud, Mergin Sina, Mark Bryant, Phil Whitaker, Martin Salley, and Bob Vogt. (S.R. Smith and SHU Sports Information.)

THE LOW POST. Seton Hall player Ricky Burton drives for inside position and an opening against a Georgetown opponent in mid-1980s action at the Meadowlands as Mike Jones (No. 4) rushes to the scene on the right wing. The Pirates had a number of other players from 1985 through 1987, including Mark Bryant, Michael Cooper, Jim Ferrer, Gerald Greene, Nick Katsikis, Khyiem Long, James Major, Andre McCloud, John Morton, Ramon Ramos, Jose Rebimbas, Martin Salley, Mergin Sina, Frank Torruella, Frantz Volcy, Daryll Walker, and Phil Whitaker. (S.R. Smith and SHU Sports Information.)

JAMES MAJOR. Major was a six-foot guard who originally hailed from Brooklyn, New York. He played for Seton Hall from 1984 through 1988 and had an all-time point total of 1,382. Included in this tally was a career high of 32 points and an arena record of 14 for 15 from the field against Rutgers in the Meadowlands on December 12, 1988, when the Pirates beat the Scarlet Knights 92-72. Seton Hall pieced together seasons of 14-18 and 15-14 between 1985 and 1987 during Major's time in uniform. Seton Hall earned a spot in the 1987 NIT. (S.R. Smith and SHU Sports Information.)

ANDRE McCLOUD. The six-foot six-inch forward puts up a reverse layup against the Villanova Wildcats during the mid-1980s as Martin Salley (No. 13) looks on from behind. McCloud was a High School All-America basketball star from Washington, D.C., who played at Seton Hall from 1982 to 1986. As a rookie with the Pirates, McCloud led the team in eight separate categories, including top scorer at 16.6 per game and rebounder with a 6.6 average. He was named a Big East All-Rookie Team selection, Rookie of the Year, and Honorable Mention Freshman All-American. An All–Big East Third Team selection in both 1984 and 1985, McCloud tallied 1,976 career points and was claimed by the Philadelphia 76ers in the sixth round of the 1985 NBA draft. (S.R. Smith and SHU Sports Information.)

MARK BRYANT. Mark Bryant was a hometown product from South Orange who attended Columbia High School and went on to play at Seton Hall from 1984 to 1988. Bryant, a six-foot nine-inch forward, was a teammate of Spencer Bryant, his brother, and together they comprised the first sibling tandem since Jim and Peter LaCorte during the early 1970s. As a newcomer, Mark was an All–Big East Freshman selection and, by 1987–1988, was named a First Team conference selection. He ended his Seton Hall career with 1,906 points prior to being selected as the No. 1 pick of the Portland Trailblazers in the 1988 draft. A 13-year NBA veteran, Mark was named to the Seton Hall Athletic Hall of Fame in 1997. (S.R. Smith and SHU Sports Information.)

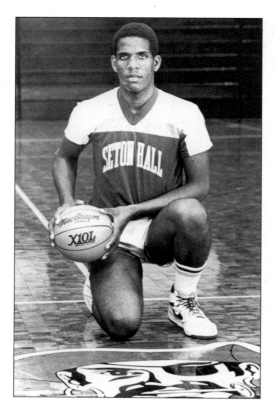

RAMON RAMOS. Recipient of the Big East Conference Scholar-Athlete award in 1989, Ramon Ramos was also chosen as a First Team All–Big East representative that same year. A native of Puerto Rico, Ramos came to New Jersey and helped to pace the Pirates from 1985 to 1989. He excelled in both the court and classroom and was an accounting major who registered 1,017 points in his career. After graduation, Ramos played for the Portland Trailblazers for a year before tragedy struck in December 1989, when he sustained head injuries in a car accident. Seton Hall annually bestows the Ramon Ramos Medal of Courage to a student "who exemplified extraordinary courage and ability in overcoming life's challenges." (S.R. Smith and SHU Sports Information.)

MARTIN SALLEY. Another star player who showed fine ball control, Martin Salley, a six-foot five-inch forward, surveys the court against an opponent in late-1980s action. Salley played for Seton Hall from 1984 to 1988 and gained distinction as team captain in 1987–1988, becoming the first Pirate cager to hold this leadership role since 1979. Salley scored 947 points in 123 career games. In 1986, Salley and his teammates were honored at the first-ever Midnight Madness held at Seton Hall. This squad also had to contend with the addition of a 45-second shot clock and potential for earning an NCAA Tournament bid that expanded its round-robin format to include 64 teams. (S.R. Smith and SHU Sports Information.)

THE 1987–1988 TEAM. This team was the first Seton Hall squad to score three-pointers, as the NCAA allowed the shot in competitive play from the 1987 season onward. Pictured here are members of the Pirate team that had its first 20-win season since 1955–1956. The roster included Mark Bryant, Michael Cooper, Gerald Greene, Nick Katsikis, Khyiem Long, James Major, John Morton, Ramon Ramos, Jose Rebimbas, Martin Salley, Quinn Smith, Frantz Volcy, Daryll Walker, and Pookey Wigington. (S.R. Smith and SHU Sports Information.)

ONE, TWO, THREE BREAK! Members of the Seton Hall squad huddle and ready themselves to resume play during this late-1980s contest. Prolific scorer Daryll Walker (second from left) played for the Pirates from 1985 to 1989 and tallied 1,022 points overall. A six-foot eight-inch forward who came to Seton Hall from New York City, Walker attended All-Hallows Academy, located in the Bronx. Seton Hall ended the 1987–1988 season with a 22-13 mark. They started the 1987 campaign with three straight victories in the Big Apple NIT tournament. Once in the NCAA Tournament, Seton Hall defeated the University of Texas, El Paso, 80-64 in the opener before bowing to the University of Arizona 84-55 in the next round. (S.R. Smith and SHU Sports Information.)

JOHN MORTON. Standing at six feet three inches tall, John Morton was also known as "Silk" for his smooth court presence in the guard position between 1985 and 1989. In high school, Morton was an All-American selection. At Seton Hall, he scored 1,621 career points and shares the school record with Gerald Greene for most games played with 131. Morton's other records include most games played in a season (38), most field goals attempted (2,166), points in a season (3,107), and free throw percentage (.756, 785-1,039) in 1988–1989. After leaving Seton Hall, Morton was chosen by the Cleveland Cavaliers in the first round of the 1989 NBA draft. (S.R. Smith and SHU Sports Information.)

ANTHONY AVENT. Avent was a six-foot nine-inch center-forward from Newark who played at Seton Hall from 1988 to 1991 and scored 1,067 career points. During his senior year, Avent received an All-American honorable mention and was selected by the Atlanta Hawks in the first round of the NBA draft. Seton Hall has had many showdowns with rival New Jersey–based NCAA Division I programs Rutgers and Princeton, as well as with Fairleigh Dickinson, Monmouth, Rider, St. Peter's, and Upsala. In 1989, however, Seton Hall would be likened to Indiana's underdog Hickory Huskers of the popular movie *Hoosiers*. (S.R. Smith and SHU Sports Information.)

Six
THE MODERN ERA
1989–2002

A SEASON TO REMEMBER. This 1988–1989 team earned its second straight NCAA Tournament bid and made a run through Southwest Missouri State 60-51, Evansville 87-73, Indiana 78-65, and UNLV 84-61. The Pirates defeated Duke in the semifinal 95-78 but lost to Michigan 80-79 in overtime, ending the season at 31-7. Pictured, from left to right, are the following: (front row) Chris Crowell (manager), Rene Monteserin, Gerald Greene, Khyiem Long, Daryll Walker, Ramon Ramos, John Morton, Pookey Wigington, Jose Rebimbas, and David Flood (manager); (back row) John Carroll (assistant coach), Rod Baker (assistant coach), Bruce Hamburger (assistant coach), Trevor Crowley, Nick Katsikis, Frantz Volcy, Anthony Avent, Andrew Gaze, Michael Cooper, Tom Sullivan (assistant coach), John Levitt (head trainer), and P.J. Carlesimo (head coach). (S.R. Smith and SHU Sports Information.)

CELEBRATION TIME! Here are some scenes from the April 6, 1989 reception in South Orange for the Seton Hall basketball team; the crowd included between 10,000 and 12,000 fans. *Upper left:* The time was declared "P.J. Carlesimo Day" and "Seton Hall Pirate Week." Here, head coach rides with John Morton at the head of the parade down South Orange Avenue. *Upper right:* Key players Ramon Ramos (left) and Andrew Gaze (right) would go on to play in the Olympics for Puerto Rico and Australia, respectively. In fact, they played against each other in the first round of the 1988 Seoul games, and Gaze carried the Australian flag at the head of his country's delegation to open the 2000 Sydney games. *Lower left:* Signing autographs and posing for pictures became the norm for the conquering heroes of the tournament. *Lower right:* A championship banner was raised to the rafters of Walsh Gymnasium during the Midnight Madness celebration of 1990. (*Galleon* yearbook.)

THE 1990–1991 TEAM. Selected as Team of the Year by the New Jersey College Coaches Association, this squad went 25-9 and earned its first-ever Big East Championship in the process. After posting a 12-16 record during the 1989–1990 season, the Pirates rebounded to defeat Clemson 78-62 and won Seton Hall's initial Big East–ACC Challenge Game. They made it to the Elite Eight of the NCAA Tournament by beating Pepperdine 71-51, Creighton 81-69, and Arizona 81-77 before falling to UNLV in the regional finals on the way to a No. 6 year-ending rank in the USA-CNN Top 25 poll. From left to right are the following: (front row) Terry Dehere, Daryl Crist, Oliver Taylor (Big East Tournament MVP), Anthony Avent, Marco Lokar, and Bryan Caver; (back row) John Leahy, Gordon Winchester, Chris Davis, Jim Dickinson, Arturas Karnishovas, Assaf Barnea, and Jerry Walker. (S.R. Smith and SHU Sports Information.)

THE 1991–1992 TEAM. This group registered a 23-9 record and earned home and away wins over traditional Big East foes St. John's, Miami, and UConn prior to a NCAA Tournament bid and first-round game against LaSalle on March 19, 1992. Seton Hall broadcaster Warner Fusselle noted that this was one of his most exciting games he ever aired as the Pirates beat the Explorers 78-76 on Terry Dehere's game winning shot with one second left in regulation. Seton Hall came back to defeat Missouri 88-71 to earn a Sweet Sixteen appearance before losing to Duke. The team ranked 18 in season-ending top 25 polls. From left to right are the following: (front row) Danny Hurley, Carlos Sanchez, Gordon Winchester, John Leahy, Terry Dehere, and Daryl Crist; (back row) Chris Davis, Arturas Karnishovas, Jim Dickinson, Luther Wright, Darrell Mims, and Jerry Walker. (S.R. Smith and SHU Sports Information.)

BIG EAST VICTORS. Members of the 1992–1993 Seton Hall Pirates celebrate after winning the Big East title by defeating Georgetown 83-69, Providence 69-60, and Syracuse 103-70, thereby earning a bid to the NCAA Tournament. After beating Tennessee State 81-59, the Pirates lost in the second round but ended the season 28-7 with a No. 6 national ranking. In the finals of the preseason NIT, the team had defeated Delaware 75-54, Tennessee 72-64, and UCLA 73-64 before losing to Indiana. The tip-off of the first Seton Hall–Meadowlands tournament was also won by the Pirates after they topped Cornell 75-59 and James Madison 87-66. (*Galleon* yearbook.)

A CHAMPIONSHIP FEELING. Pictured are the senior members of the Seton Hall Big East Championship team. From left to right, Terry Dehere, Daryl Crist, and Jerry Walker raise the trophy at center court of Madison Square Garden on March 14, 1993. Tournament MVP Terry Dehere led the Pirates along with Luther Wright, who would go on to be a first-round selection of the Utah Jazz in the 1993 NBA draft. Rounding out membership on the 1992–1993 squad were Bryan Caver, Daryl Crist, Chris Davis, Terry Dehere, Jim Dickinson, Craig Duerksen, Adrian Griffin, Danny Hurley, Arturas Karnishovas, John Leahy, Darrell Mims, Tchaka Shipp, Jerry Walker, and Luther Wright. (S.R. Smith and SHU Sports Information.)

TERRY DEHERE. Dehere was the first Seton Hall basketball star to have his number (24) retired as an active player and became the first sophomore to surpass the 1,000-point mark. He is the all-time leading scorer in school history with 2,494 points. Dehere came to Seton Hall from St. Anthony's High School in Jersey City. Upon graduation, he earned a spot on the Pirate varsity, where he played from 1989 to 1993 and led the team in scoring all four years. Along with his scoring ability, Dehere is the Seton Hall career leader in games started (128), minutes played (4,272), and three-pointers attempted and made (315 of 809). Dehere is the second all-time leading scorer in Big East Conference history as of the 2001–2002 season. He earned Big East Player of the Year and Tournament MVP laurels along with being named a Consensus All-American selection in 1993. Dehere earned a bronze medal as part of the 1991 U.S. Pan-American Games team and was named Seton Hall Athlete of the Year in both 1992 and 1993 before being selected 13th in the 1993 NBA draft by the Los Angeles Clippers. Dehere has played with the Sacramento Kings and Vancouver Grizzlies during the course of his professional career. (S.R. Smith and SHU Sports Information.)

DEHERE DRIVES. A familiar pose during the early 1990s shows Terry Dehere making his way to the basket. Even though Dehere graduated in 1993, the team went 17-13 during the 1993–1994 season. Included on this team were Andre Brown, Dwight Brown, Bryan Caver, Chris Davis, Adrian Griffin, Danny Hurley, Arturas Karnishovas, John Leahy, Darrell Mims, Chris Morrison, Tchaka Shipp, and John Yablonski. Danny Hurley was a six-foot two-inch guard whose father, Bob Hurley, coached him at St. Anthony's High School in Jersey City. Hurley scored 1,070 points during his Seton Hall career, which lasted from 1991 to 1996. (S.R. Smith and SHU Sports Information.)

ARTURAS KARNISHOVAS. The 1993 and 1994 Big East Scholar-Athlete of the Year Award Winner was Arturas Karnishovas, a six-foot eight-inch forward from Vilnius, Lithuania. Karnishovas was among the first international players to represent Seton Hall on the court and one of the earliest Soviets to play American college basketball. He played for the Pirates from 1990 to 1994 and amassed 1,509 career points. Karnishovas was on the bronze medal Lithuanian National Team in the 1992 Olympics. In 1994, Karnishovas was named to the GT/COSIDA Academic All-American Team prior to playing professional basketball in Europe. (S.R. Smith and SHU Sports Information.)

JERRY WALKER. Named Big East Defensive Player of the Year in 1993, Jerry Walker is shown putting up a jump shot against Georgetown. He scored 1,075 points and had 104 blocked shots in 99 games between 1990 and 1993. Walker helped pace the Pirates during the early 1990s, and Seton Hall put together consecutive winning records of 17-13 and 16-14 between 1993 and 1995. (S.R. Smith and SHU Sports Information.)

ADRIAN GRIFFIN. Seton Hall player Adrian Griffin (No. 4) fights for position against Rutgers at the Meadowlands in this mid-1990s contest prior to the introduction of the 35-second shot clock introduced in 1994. Griffin played for the Pirates from 1992 to 1996 and scored 1,414 points over his career before being named Big East Scholar-Athlete of the Year in 1996. Between 1995 and 1997, Seton Hall featured a roster of solid performers, including Sean Codey, John Fairchild, Adrian Griffin, Shaheen Holloway, Danny Hurley, Roger Ingraham, John Johnson, Duane Jordan, Jacky Kaba, Rimas Kaukenas, Roy Leath, Mark Morrison, Kelland Payton, Levell Sanders, Bayonne Taty, Donnell Williams, and John Yablonski. (S.R. Smith and SHU Sports Information.)

GEORGE BLANEY. George Blaney is kneeling in the center with the 1994–1995 Pirates, his first team, which went 16-14 on the season. He was named head coach on July 22, 1994, after playing for the Philadelphia 76ers and New York Knicks and heading the basketball team at his alma mater, Holy Cross, for the previous 27 years. A product of New Jersey, Blaney said the first game he ever saw was at Walsh Gymnasium. He won over 400 games as a college coach and had a 38-48 record at Seton Hall, including 12-16 and 10-18 marks between 1995 and 1997. The 1994–1996 team featured Andre Brown, Dwight Brown, Chris Davis, John Fairchild, Andre Griffin, Bruce Hamburger (assistant coach), Greg Herenda (assistant coach), Danny Hurley, Roger Ingraham, Jacky Kaba, John Leahy, Levell Sanders, Jerwaun Tuck, Donnell Williams, Kenny Williamson (assistant coach), and John Yablonski. (S.R. Smith and SHU Sports Information.)

SHAHEEN HOLLOWAY. This three-time All–Big East selection and scorer of 1,588 career points was a star player for the Pirates between 1996 and 2000. Holloway was named the most improved player in the Big East for the 2000 season, a year in which Seton Hall went to the NCAA Tournament. Seton Hall broadcaster Warner Fusselle noted that March 17 was indeed a "Green Day" because Holloway and teammate Samuel Dalembert were graduates of St. Patrick's High School and were playing an Oregon team that wore emerald-colored uniforms on St. Patrick's Day no less! The proverbial luck of the Irish for Seton Hall was evident as Holloway put in a length-of-the-court layup with 1.9 seconds left to defeat the Ducks in overtime 72-71. (S.R. Smith and SHU Sports Information.)

TOMMY AMAKER. A player and former assistant coach at Duke University from 1983 to 1997, Tommy Amaker became one of the youngest head coaches in Seton Hall basketball history when he was hired on March 19, 1997. Amaker noted in his press conference, "I'm extremely flattered and honored to have an opportunity to represent such a prestigious university with a rich basketball tradition." Amaker amassed a 68-55 record between 1997 and 2000, including four winning seasons of 15-15 from 1997 to 1999, 22-10 in 1999–2000, and 16-15 a year later with such players as Eddie Griffin and Samuel Dalembert, who entered the NBA draft in 2001. Seton Hall went to the 2000 NCAA Tournament but also earned three NIT bids during the Amaker era. (*Galleon* yearbook.)

CLOCK WATCHING. Seton Hall players anxiously look up to see how much time remains in a late-1990s game against St. Peter's at the Meadowlands. The players on Pirate squads between 1997 and 1999 included Brian Campbell, Ramon Cespedes, Damian Dawkins, Reggie Garrett, Shaheen Holloway, John Johnson, Duane Jordan, Jacky Kaba, Rimas Kaukenas, Charles Manga, Chuck Moore, Levell Sanders, Gary Saunders, Donnell Williams, and Ty Shine. Many of these Pirates also represented the university in the midst of crisis. On January 19, 2000, Seton Hall suffered a dormitory fire that resulted in the loss of three lives. This tragedy overwhelmed the campus and community alike. (*Galleon* yearbook.)

THE 1999–2000 TEAM. Seton Hall's NCAA Sweet Sixteen squad of 1999–2000 went 22-10 on the year. Pictured, from left to right, are the following: (front row) Kevin Wilkins, Ryan Peterson, Ty Shine, Shaheen Holloway (co-captain), Gary Saunders, Rimas Kaukenas (co-captain), Brian Campbell, Reggie Garrett, Darius Lane, and Desmond Herod; (back row) Kirsten Green (director of basketball operations), Eric Leibler (staff assistant), Michael Oakes (administrative assistant), Chris Collins (assistant coach), Damian Dawkins, Al Harris, Charles Manga, Samuel Dalembert, Greg Morton, Tommy Amaker (head coach), Rob Jackson (assistant coach), Fred Hill (assistant coach), Phil Dyer (coordinator of strength and conditioning), Joe Vignier (head manager), and Sheila Noecker (assistant athletic trainer). (S.R. Smith and SHU Sports Information.)

RALLY STUDENTS OF SETONIA. In the wake of the 2000 dorm fire tragedy, the Seton Hall basketball team provided inspiration, as athletic director Jeff Fogelson related in retrospect: "There were no standout players but rather their success was the result of everyone complimenting each other. . . . It provided an opportunity for the Seton Hall community which had been joined together in grief for nearly two months to rejoice as one in the team's success. The NCAA Tournament became a step in the healing process and this is its meaningful legacy." After defeating Oregon in the first round of the 2000 NCAA Tournament, Seton Hall opposed fifth nationally ranked Temple. Seton Hall broadcaster Warner Fusselle's comment "an upset of biblical proportions" proved prophetic, and Seton Hall defeated Temple in overtime 67-65. (*Galleon* yearbook.)

THE FUTURE. The Pirates entered this new century on April 4, 2001, as Louis Orr (pictured in the center with Msgr. Robert Sheeran, president of Seton Hall University, and wife Yvette Orr) was hired as the 17th head coach in program history. Orr played at Syracuse from 1976 through 1980 and in the NBA for eight seasons. He noted, "Seton Hall has a very long and rich tradition of excellence for more than 50 years. From NIT championship game participants to 2 Big East championships, Seton Hall Basketball has had more than its share of success. We want to build a foundation for the present and the future that successfully combines winning character, winning academics and winning basketball in a family atmosphere. We are building a program that will be consistently successful in all areas. We are excited about the present and the future. We hope to build on our steep tradition." Msgr. Robert Sheeran, university president, also summed up what Seton Hall basketball means to the school. "A strong athletic program generates energy and excitement: It's good for our students—and good for the University. At our Seton Hall basketball games—both men's and women's—there is a real sense of community. Our pride in the Pirates and our pride in the University draws us together. It's a great feeling." (S.R. Smith and SHU Sports Information.)

BIBLIOGRAPHY

Bee, Clair. *Backboard Fever*. New York: Grosset & Dunlap, 1953.
————. *Championship Ball*. New York: Grosset & Dunlap, 1948.
————. *Hoop Crazy*. New York: Grosset & Dunlap, 1950.
Bjarkman, Peter C. *Hoopla: A Century of College Basketball*. Indianapolis, Indiana: Masters Press, 1996.
————. *The Biographical History of Basketball*. Lincolnwood, Illinois: Masters Press, 2000.
Cunningham, Thomas W., ed. *The Summit of a Century: The Centennial Story of Seton Hall University, 1856–1956*. South Orange, New Jersey: Seton Hall University, 1956.
Devaney, John. *The Story of Basketball*. New York: Random House, 1976.
Galleon yearbook. South Orange, New Jersey: Seton Hall College-University, 1947–1999.
Hobson, Howard A. *Scientific Basketball for Coaches, Players, Officials, Spectators, and Sportswriters*. New York: Prentice-Hall, 1949.
Hollander, Zander, ed. *The Modern Encyclopedia of Basketball*. New York: Four Winds Press, 1973.
Men's Basketball Radio-TV-Media Guide. South Orange, New Jersey: Seton Hall College-University, 1946–2002.
NCAA Basketball's Finest: All Time Greatest Men's Collegiate Players and Coaches. Overland Park, Kansas: National Collegiate Athletic Association, 1991.
Russell, John. *Honey Russell: Between Games, Between Halves*. Washington, D.C.: Dryad Press, 1986.
Seton Hall College Catalog. South Orange, New Jersey: Seton Hall College, 1899–1949.
Seton Hall University Athletics-Basketball Manuscript-Photograph-Scrapbook Collection, 1903–2002. Record Groups 0 & 13. Msgr. William Noé Field Archives & Special Collections Center. South Orange, New Jersey: Seton Hall University.
Setonian student newspaper. South Orange, New Jersey: Seton Hall University, 1924–2002.
Stewart, Mark. *Basketball: A History of Hoops*. New York: Franklin Watts, 1998.
Vitale, Dick, and Curry Kirkpatrick. *Vitale*. New York: Simon and Schuster, 1988.
Vitale, Dick, and Dick Weiss. *Holding Court: Reflections on the Game I Love*. Indianapolis, Indiana: Masters Press, 1995.
White and Blue yearbook. South Orange, New Jersey: Seton Hall College, 1924–1942.

CHEER, CHEER FOR OLD SETON HALL! A whimsical sketch of the student body is shown in full voice, waving banners as they root on their alma mater. This type of chic cartoon was in vogue for college annuals during the early decades of the 20th century, but school spirit has always been evident at the Catholic university in New Jersey since the founding of Seton Hall in 1856 to the present day. (SHU Archives.)